Making Teaching Community Property

A Menu for Peer Collaboration and Peer Review

BY PAT HUTCHINGS

Director, AAHE Teaching Initiative

AAHE TEACHING INITIATIVE

American Association for Higher Education

Acknowledgments

Funding to produce this volume was provided by The William and Flora Hewlett Foundation and The Pew Charitable Trusts, which also jointly fund the project on which it is based: "From Idea to Prototype: The Peer Review of Teaching."

Many individuals contributed to this volume in ways indicated in the preface and introduction. I would also like to acknowledge the considerable contribution from the University of Wyoming, where I spent the 1995-96 academic year as visiting professor, and where most of the work on the book was completed. Finally, I'd like to thank my good colleagues at AAHE, and especially Bry Pollack, director of publications, who managed the production of the book through many long-distance transactions between Washington, DC and Laramie, Wyoming.

—*PH*

Deborah DeZure's Faculty Report in Chapter 2 was excerpted with permission from "Opening the Classroom Door," *Academe,* September-October 1993. © 1993 American Association of University Professors.

"The Muddiest Point: A Simple But Powerful Classroom Assessment Technique" (Chapter 4, p. 42) was excerpted with permission from *Classroom Assessment Techniques: A Handbook for College Teachers,* 2nd ed., by Thomas A. Angelo and K. Patricia Cross. © 1993 Jossey-Bass Inc., Publishers.

"A Protocol for Interviewing Students" (Chapter 4, p. 39) was excerpted with permission from *Assessing Faculty Work: Enhancing Individual and Institutional Performance,* by Larry A. Braskamp and John C. Ory. © 1994 Jossey-Bass Inc., Publishers.

"Adapting the Muddiest Point Technique" (Chapter 4, p. 43) was excerpted with permission from "'The Muddiest Point in the Lecture' as a Feedback Device," *On Teaching and Learning,* April 1989. © 1989 Harvard University.

Making Teaching Community Property: A Menu for Peer Collaboration and Peer Review
by Pat Hutchings

For more about the AAHE Teaching Initiative, see pp. 107-109. For more about AAHE's project "From Idea to Prototype: The Peer Review of Teaching," see pp. 111-115. Additional copies of this publication are available from AAHE Publications. For ordering information, contact:

AMERICAN ASSOCIATION FOR HIGHER EDUCATION
One Dupont Circle, Suite 360
Washington, DC 20036-1110
ph 202/293-6440   fax 202/293-0073   ISBN 1-56377-031-8

TABLE OF CONTENTS

Faculty Report: "Setting a Scholarly Tone: Teaching Circles in the History
Department at Kent State University"
John Jameson
Faculty Report: "Fostering Collective Responsibility for Student Learning:
Teaching Seminars in the University of North Carolina at Charlotte
Mathematics Department"
Charles Burnap and Miriam Leiva
Faculty Report: "Learning Together: An Online Faculty Conversation
About Online Student Conversation at Rio Hondo College"
Susan Obler

Faculty Report: "Reciprocal Classroom Visits: An Experiment in the
Temple University History Department"
William Cutler and Howard Spodek
Faculty Report: "The Teacher Observation/Peer Support (TOPS) Program at
California State University-Dominguez Hills"
Kathleen McEnerney and Jamie L. Webb
Faculty Report: "The Featured Faculty Program at Eastern Michigan
University"
Deborah DeZure

Faculty Report: "A New Faculty Mentoring Program in the Stanford
English Department"
David Halliburton
Faculty Report: "The Faculty Tutorial Program at Saint Olaf College"
Jonathan Hill
Faculty Report: "The Issue of Supply: Fostering Senior Faculty Leadership
at The College of Saint Catherine"
Marilou Eldred

Faculty Report: "Interviewing Each Other's Students in the Legal Studies
Program at the University of Georgia"
Peter Shedd
Faculty Report: "Classroom Assessment as a Context for Faculty
Conversation and Collaboration at California State University-Long
Beach"
Susan Nummedal
Faculty Report: "Making Students More Active Agents in Their Learning:
TQM in the Syracuse University School of Business"
Frances Zollers

Faculty Report: "Inventing a New Genre: The Course Portfolio at the
University of Wisconsin-La Crosse"
William Cerbin

P R E F A C E

This book began, for me, at a meeting in January 1994 at the Hyatt Regency Hotel in New Orleans. Pat Hutchings and I looked at each other with a mixture of elation and apprehension as the participants gathered for a special meeting during AAHE's Conference on Faculty Roles & Rewards. Seated around the table were provosts and other representatives from twelve universities, senior program officers from The William and Flora Hewlett Foundation and The Pew Charitable Trusts, and Lee Shulman, Charles Ducommun Professor of Education at Stanford University. Before each of us was a sixty-three-page grant proposal Pat and I had written titled "From Idea to Prototype: The Peer Review of Teaching."

Pat's and my elation came from having assembled the key ingredients for change: some exciting ideas about an approach to educational improvement, top administrators strongly committed to the ideas, and foundation partners who had not only promised support but had themselves made important contributions to project design. The scary part was that, as authors of the proposal, we weren't sure what the promised "prototypes" of the project's title might look like. We were making a leap of faith that "out there," on the campuses represented around the room, were faculty who not only would volunteer to engage the work of the project but would actually invent new ways that teaching could be peer reviewed. As one of those faculty later said, that task was like "trying to write a short story before the genre had been invented." Though there are established conventions for sharing the fruits of research, academe has not developed parallel vehicles for making teaching (as Lee Shulman puts it) "community property."

It is, in fact, largely Lee's research and thinking about teaching that provides the intellectual foundation for the project that resulted from that proposal. In studies of outstanding K-12 teachers, Lee had found that high-quality teaching was a subtle and complex process — a process requiring both a deep understanding of a particular field of knowledge and a capacity to transform this knowledge (with analogies, demonstrations, and the like) in ways that connect with students' diverse mental worlds.

These findings were not themselves surprising. But as Lee pointed out, they *contradicted* the conception of teaching that is pervasive throughout schools, colleges, and universities — the conception of teaching as technique, as learning the "how to's" of lecturing and managing discussion groups, etc.

For us at AAHE, Lee's message was like a star shell bursting in the night, suddenly illuminating a new way of thinking about how to improve the quality of higher education. It explained the curious phenomenon we had observed so often: that even faculty who care deeply about their own teaching rarely regard teaching as an intellectual endeavor worthy of reading, systematic inquiry, or even conversation. Lee helped us see that the neglect of teaching as an intellectual topic might be rooted not in anything intrinsic to the nature of teaching but in the *conception* of teaching that had come to dominate our thinking. The problem, as Pogo would say, was us!

This implied an exciting line of work for AAHE's Teaching Initiative. If we could introduce faculty to a conception of teaching that honored faculty's intuitive appreciation for the subtle processes of "knowledge transformation" entailed in quality teaching, then perhaps teaching *could* become a subject of ongoing professional, collegial discourse. A culture of interest in teaching could develop that would contain its own dynamic for continual improvement.

Indeed, as we came to appreciate what Lee had articulated about the kind of knowing that goes into quality teaching, we realized that he was also guiding us through and beyond the sterile debates about teaching versus research, and what curriculum was essential. If teaching entailed the transformation of knowledge, then teaching and research were two sides of the same coin — the coin of scholarship. If teaching entailed the transformation of knowledge, then the question of what subjects should be taught couldn't be settled without reference to considering *how* these subjects were taught. Content and process, curriculum and pedagogy, had, like Humpty Dumpty, to be put back together again.

Moreover, if teaching were to be seen as scholarly, intellectual work, it would not be enough to evaluate teaching simply by looking at student ratings. Teaching, like research, should be peer reviewed. Indeed, *until* teaching is peer reviewed, it will never be truly valued.

This, then, was the premise around which the group was gathered on that January afternoon in New Orleans . . . and, after the introductions had been made, the critical issue quickly surfaced. Many of the provosts around the table had signed on for one clear reason — to improve the quality of evidence about teaching that appears in promotion/tenure files. But others around the table, and many faculty who later joined the project, argued that the endeavor should not be tied too closely to formal evaluation. For some, the concept of "peer review" put the cart before the horse. The real point, they argued, and what was needed before taking on the formal evaluation of teaching, was to develop habits and practices of faculty collaboration that would lead to genuine improvement in teaching and learning.

Fortunately, the latter view won the day. The provosts listened and agreed that the place to *start* was to initiate ways to rebuild a culture of interest in teaching. I say "fortunately" for two reasons. First, it's clear that some of the faculty who became engaged would never have done so had we started off with an agenda of improving documentation for formal review. Second, as Pat Hutchings points out in her conclusion to this book, the process of experimenting with colleagues in the name of improvement has yielded ideas that are relevant and useful for formal evaluation.

Each of the provosts agreed that January afternoon to sponsor faculty from three pilot departments to work on the project. The faculty (typically two per department) spent an intensive week at Stanford University in June of 1994, developing plans for pilot projects that they then pursued over the course of the following year. In June 1995, they all met again at Georgetown University to share their work.

The enthusiasm those faculty brought to the Georgetown event, and the early fruits of their work, was something we all thought just had to be shared. So we persuaded Pat Hutchings to take on the task of representing the work of the project to a broader audience. Pat brought to the task not only her "project central" understandings and her connections to all the faculty who were working as part of the project, but her special gifts as an English professor and writer, who loves teaching and finds delight in sharing good news about what works.

Pat would be the first to say that the real authors of this book are the faculty who first did the work and then took the time to collaborate with her in telling their stories to others. As the book took shape, her search for examples led beyond the project campuses to other campus settings. We are grateful to all the faculty who contributed.

In the course of this project, our foundation partners — Ray Bacchetti, Robert Schwartz, and Ellen Wert — have become not just program officers but colleagues and coparticipants. Lee Shulman has become not just our intellectual guide but a marvelous colleague and friend. Many of the faculty we've worked with will remain colleagues and friends long after the project is over. Collaboration about teaching is good for teaching. It's also good for the soul.

Russell Edgerton
President, American Association for Higher Education
March 1996

INTRODUCTION

"I NOW BELIEVE THAT THE REASON TEACHING IS NOT MORE VALUED IN THE
ACADEMY IS BECAUSE THE WAY WE TREAT TEACHING REMOVES IT FROM THE
COMMUNITY OF SCHOLARS."

— Lee Shulman (1993), p. 6

AAHE's Teaching Initiative is a program dedicated to the idea of creating a
"culture of teaching and learning," and *Making Teaching Community Property*
is about ways to do that. As Russ Edgerton's preface suggests, this volume
comes out of a particular context of work — a twelve-university project, entitled From Idea to Prototype: The Peer Review of Teaching — and it was the
experience of faculty participating in that project that led us to publish it. But
the vision behind the chapters that follow here is relevant, we believe, on all
campuses: that teaching, like other forms of scholarly activity, is substantive,
intellectual work. That is, teaching is a matter not simply of method and
technique (though these are the aspects of teaching that have received the
most attention) but of selecting, organizing, and transforming one's field so
that it can be engaged and understood at a deep level by students. Like scholarly research, our courses are acts of intellectual invention, and our teaching
of those courses enacts the ways we think about and pursue our fields of
study. Seen in this way, the work of teaching — as Lee Shulman says — right-
ly belongs to and requires the attention of the community of scholars.

Such is the vision of the AAHE project on peer review, and of this volume, and my purpose in this introduction is to make explicit three corollar-
ies to this central vision that run as themes through the chapters that follow.
I'll also say a bit about what you'll find in those chapters, how they're organized, and how to take advantage of the resources they offer.

TEACHING AS SCHOLARLY WORK: THREE COROLLARIES

First, to call teaching scholarly work is to see it as **a process of ongoing
inquiry and reflection.** It is to assert that teaching is a matter not simply of
standing and delivering (no matter how skillfully or with what eloquence)
but also of examining and advancing one's knowledge and practice. Pointing
to the need for "teachers as scholars," K. Patricia Cross (1990) notes, "the
intellectual challenge of teaching lies in the opportunity for individual teachers to observe the impact of their teaching on their students' learning. And
yet, most of us don't use our classrooms as laboratories for the study of learning" (p. 3).

Cross's point is echoed by William Cutler, whose report appears in
Chapter 2. Recounting his experience of reciprocal classroom visits undertaken with a colleague in the history department at Temple University, Cutler
notes, "Teaching tends to get turned into a routine. . . . So it's a good idea no
matter how experienced you are, and how well things seem to be working in
the classroom, to step back and examine your teaching and your students'

learning."

In fact, it is this need to "step back and examine" that stands behind many of the strategies featured in this volume — be they reciprocal classroom visits, protocols for interviewing each other's students, or course portfolios; they are antidotes to the daily grind, windows into new pedagogical ideas and insights. They are, as the Faculty Reports in subsequent chapters suggest, badly needed occasions for a kind of reflection and inquiry that is essential to what it means to see and undertake teaching as scholarly work.

A second corollary to a view of teaching as scholarly work is **the need for collegial exchange and publicness.** In a wonderful essay entitled "Teaching Alone, Learning Together," Lee Shulman (1988) points up just how hard it is, in the booming, buzzing confusion of the classroom, for faculty to *see* themselves as teachers, and therefore to know what and how to improve; what's needed, Shulman contends, is assistance from colleagues who can help them do so. Faculty Reports in this volume constitute a running reprise on Shulman's point, showing over and over, in various contexts, that working together around issues of teaching and learning is just plain helpful; that there are aspects of teaching that faculty peers are best (or particularly well) equipped to assist with.

One obvious example relates to course content: Is the material current with the field? Is it the most important material for the students in the course? Are examples apt and telling? Is the course pitched at the right level of difficulty? Is student work evaluated appropriately, given the standards of the field? . . . These are aspects of teaching where collegial exchange with peers in one's own field is highly beneficial. I think here, for instance, of a comment by one of the mathematicians in the AAHE peer review of teaching project, who told me, "Peers from the field are even more crucial than I first thought." And I think of the experience of two faculty from a pilot department in the project who interviewed each other's students (see Chapter 4). "There really is something to this peer stuff," one of them said afterward. "You learn things together you can't learn alone."

Moreover, the benefits of and rationale for these kinds of peer collaboration are more than just immediately practical ones. When Joy Ritchie and her Department of English colleague at the University of Nebraska-Lincoln undertake a collaborative study of their theory and practice as teachers of composition, they do so not only to learn something useful for the next semester but to fulfill a responsibility to their scholarly community and to enact that community's emerging conception of teaching: "Good teaching and good theory, as bell hooks reminds us in *Teaching to Transgress,* are always collaborative," they argue in Chapter 7. "Thus, we want to emphasize that this collaboration is not something we've undertaken because it's currently fashionable; nor was it undertaken merely in the service of institutional or professional goals. Our collaboration emerges directly and intrinsically from our philosophies about teaching and research as fundamentally dialogical activities."

The third corollary of teaching as scholarly work is that faculty take **professional responsibility for the quality of their work as teachers.** In the context of research, faculty belong to scholarly communities that serve to set standards for the field — not in rigid exclusionary fashion, but as a constant process of defining and redefining the field, identifying and addressing its major issues, determining what's important, making judgments about work that is (and is not) seminal.

In the context of teaching, however, there is no such process of collective standard setting yet. On most campuses, the evaluation of teaching is something that happens *to* faculty; they are objects, not agents, of the process. Some faculty no doubt prefer it this way; one I met at a recent conference told me, with some anger, that the evaluation of teaching was "an administrator's job" and should not be "laid on faculty."

But if, as is assumed in the chapters that follow here, teaching is a scholarly activity, with all that implies, then faculty must play a central role in ensuring and improving its quality. Doing so is a professional responsibility, quaint as it may sound to say so, and it's also a practical necessity. For if faculty do not take charge of ensuring (and setting the standards for) the quality of teaching, bureaucratic forms of accountability from outside academe will surely rule the day.

To put all of this a different way, the "problem" this volume attempts to address is not that the state of teaching is bad and needs to be fixed, not that there aren't plenty of good and dedicated teachers out there. The problem is the lack of a campus culture in which the quality and improvement of teaching are subjects of ongoing collective faculty attention and responsibility.

A MENU OF STRATEGIES FOR MAKING TEACHING COMMUNITY PROPERTY

The good news is that many faculty would and do welcome ways to be more public and collegial about their teaching and their students' learning — and the purpose of this volume is to set forth, in practical, useful terms, strategies that move us toward Lee Shulman's vision of teaching as "community property."

The book is organized into nine chapters, each focused on a particular strategy (or category of strategies) for peer collaboration. It is, if you will, a kind of menu.

And like a menu, which conveniently separates the appetizers from entrees, the salads from desserts, this volume, too, does some sorting for you. It begins with strategies that are — relatively speaking, at least — more modest, more immediately doable: things such as "teaching circles" (Chapter 1) and reciprocal classroom visits (Chapter 2) that can be done in small doses, once or twice a semester, for a few hours. As the Faculty Reports of those strategies indicate, real benefits can result from their use, but they're fairly simple in the sense that a small group of interested individuals can, without trying to bring whole departments on board or getting tangled up in issues of institutional policy, "just do it" . . . and of course we hope the examples and suggestions included here will make that doing even easier and more appealing.

Later chapters, by contrast, focus on more elaborate, and by some measure more ambitious, forms of collaboration. Chapter 6, for instance, looks beyond the episodic exchanges featured earlier to the more sustained collaboration required in team teaching and teaching teams, such as the "coordinated studies" model described by Jean MacGregor, in which two or three faculty design and teach as a team an interdisciplinary course that constitutes full-time enrollment for students for that semester. Similarly, Chapter 7 features examples of collaborative inquiry and pedagogical scholarship — complex, theory-based projects on which faculty work together over a semester or more, and about which they write together. Chapter 8, in contrast to virtually all the examples in previous chapters, explores the possibilities for collaboration through formal departmental occasions and processes — collaborations that therefore require (and this is a source of their strength) consensus making and attention to matters of departmental policy.

Finally, Chapter 9 moves from collaboration that is for the most part local, to intercampus (and therefore, these days, often electronic, online) collaboration, looking as well at the possibilities for external peer review of teaching that a number of faculty in AAHE's project have told us must be a goal if teaching is ever to be valued on a par with research.

It is important to say that there is no hierarchy of value implied in the arrangement of chapters; the strategies featured in Chapter 1 — as the Faculty Reports there testify — are equally as powerful as those in Chapter 9; the issue is not finding the best strategy but finding what best meets the need at hand and most closely matches local circumstances. It should also perhaps be said that the nine chapters are not so neat as the previous paragraphs may suggest; the categories overlap in all kinds of ways: Several of the programs featured in Chapter 2 on reciprocal visits and classroom observations also entail aspects of mentoring and coaching that are featured in Chapter 3; Chapter 4 points to collaborations focused on the investigation of student learning — but you'll find instances of this focus in virtually all of the other chapters, as well. And as indicated in the conclusion, some of the strategies described in the context of collaboration may also be relevant to more formal peer review of teaching.

Finally, it's important to say that the strategies featured here are not intended as an exhaustive listing of everything possible. Many useful things are left out, and only a small sampling of examples is included. Our intent has been to put forward possibilities that are interesting, varied, complementary (doing several is more powerful than any single one), useful, and — to return to the menu metaphor — even, we hope, tasty.

HOW TO USE THIS VOLUME

As *Making Teaching Community Property* evolved, I often thought of it as a kind of handbook, and the term, while not quite apt, suggests something about how to use it, for the chapters that follow here are meant more as resources — places to go for assistance as the need arises, possibilities to browse through — than as cover-to-cover reading. And we've tried to build into each chapter a set of elements that will make your browsing profitable.

As indicated above, each chapter focuses on a particular strategy for peer collaboration around teaching and learning. Each begins with a brief set of introductory, context-setting remarks, and each concludes with a listing of resources for further work. Many of the chapters also contain tips and suggestions for successfully implementing the strategy in question. But the heart of each chapter is **reports by faculty** who have actually used (and in some cases invented) the strategies, and who recount exactly what they did, why, how it worked, and what they learned that might assist others. Several points of explanation about these Faculty Reports may be useful.

First, the Faculty Reports are drawn from a range of institutions, from community colleges to large research institutions, from private liberal arts colleges to state colleges and universities. A range of disciplines is represented, as well. But it is no accident that about half of the reports are from faculty who have been active in the AAHE project on the peer review of teaching; tipping the volume in this direction is our way of attempting to meet the many requests we receive for information on the project's developments and findings.

Second, many of the Faculty Reports (particularly those coming out of the AAHE project) are department- or program-based. This is not to suggest that crossdisciplinary collaborations are not highly powerful (you'll find examples of these, too), but it *is* to suggest that content — the "stuff" of teaching — is a powerful context for collaboration. It's significant in this regard that Jean MacGregor, in her account of interdisciplinary learning communities in Chapter 6, says "What we have found is that it is around content that faculty may feel most excited about collaborating. The best conversations begin not around a teaching method ('let's try using student groups') but around ideas that people care about . . . around the invention of the experience they want to give students in terms of content and ideas." This emphasis on content rather than method, on substance rather than only the technique of teaching, follows from the vision of teaching as scholarly work.

Finally, the faculty whose reports appear in this volume would, I'm sure, be the first to insist that they do not have all the answers; that their collaboration is a work in progress. Many talk not only about successes but very candidly about what did not work well and about issues they are still struggling with. The candor and generosity with which they share their work is in fact a further enactment of their commitment to making teaching community property . . . and a contribution for which they deserve our real gratitude. A special thanks to them all.

AN EVOLVING CONVERSATION

As this volume goes to press, the AAHE project on the peer review of teaching moves into a next stage of work. As in the work to date, we will be seeking ways to disseminate results "in process" (rather than waiting until the end to issue a final report), and we're eager to hear from campuses of all types, and faculty in all fields, about how the ideas of peer collaboration and review "play" in their settings. (For more about AAHE's peer review project, see pp. 111-115.)

In particular, we invite you to be part of what we hope will be an evolving conversation about the strategies for making teaching community property that are featured in the chapters that follow. So let us hear from you about what's useful, what's not, what other good ideas should be "on the menu," and what next challenges and opportunities you see. You'll find discussion about this last point in the conclusion, which looks at how the experience of peer collaboration can help shape more useful ways of reviewing and evaluating teaching.

RESOURCES

Cross, K. Patricia. "Teachers as Scholars." *AAHE Bulletin* 43 (4): 3-5 (December 1990).

Shulman, Lee S. "Teaching as Community Property: Putting an End to Pedagogical Solitude." *Change* 25 (6): 6-7 (November/December 1993).

————— . "Teaching Alone, Learning Together: An Agenda for Reform." In *Schooling for Tomorrow: Directing Reform to Issues That Count,* edited by T.J. Sergiovanni and J.H. Moore, pp. 166-187. Boston: Allyn and Bacon, 1988.

CHAPTER 1

TEACHING CIRCLES: STARTING THE CONVERSATION

Even on campuses where good teaching is a top priority, faculty I talk with report an experience that Lee Shulman calls "pedagogical solitude" — a state of affairs in which that aspect of faculty work that would *seem* to be the most social, the most public, turns out in fact to be the most unrelievedly private. Maybe there's occasional, desultory chat about teaching in the elevator or faculty dining room, but when it comes to planned, purposeful conversation — occasions *set aside* for good talk about good teaching (and meaningful student learning) — the situation is pretty bleak. In such circumstances, teaching circles are a wonderful way to get the conversation started.

This chapter provides a quick overview of teaching circles, followed by reports from several faculty who have found them useful in starting a conversation about teaching and learning that would not otherwise take place. You'll also find suggestions for using teaching circles, and for adapting the model to different disciplines. Additional brief examples and a list of resources round out the chapter.

WHAT IS A TEACHING CIRCLE?

The term "teaching circles" originated at the University of Nebraska, where psychology professor Daniel Bernstein coined the phrase ("I was intrigued with Japanese quality circles at the time," he explains) and pioneered their use (see Resources). Today, and in this chapter, the term is used to describe a variety of arrangements through which (1) a small group of faculty members (typically four to ten, though one example included below is larger than this) (2) makes a commitment to work together over a period of at least a semester (3) to address questions and concerns about the particulars of their teaching and their students' learning.

Structured along these general lines, teaching circles can serve individual faculty needs or advance more explicitly shared agendas — for instance, the teaching of first-year students (the topic of a long-standing teaching-circle-like group at Alverno College) or the teaching of large classes (the focus of a group at the University of Georgia). (See boxes.)

Beyond good, practical conversation, teaching-circle members might set themselves additional tasks. They might, for instance, help one another develop portfolios for use in promotion and tenure decisions; they might work together to preserve and document their conversations for a larger audience by developing a *"collective* course portfolio" (see Steve Dunbar's report in Chapter 6), or by developing a departmental teaching library (see Chapter 8). Teaching circles might also conduct cooperative assessment of student learning, as in the example below from Rio Hondo College.

The specific activities and arrangements, as well as the names of these collaborative, practice-centered groups (several of the examples below do not use the term "teaching circle"), vary with context and purpose. Indeed, a

"WE CLOSE THE CLASSROOM DOOR AND EXPERIENCE PEDAGOGICAL SOLITUDE, WHEREAS IN OUR LIFE AS SCHOLARS, WE ARE MEMBERS OF ACTIVE COMMUNITIES: COMMUNITIES OF CONVERSATION, COMMUNITIES OF EVALUATION, COMMUNITIES IN WHICH WE GATHER WITH OTHERS IN OUR INVISIBLE COLLEGES TO EXCHANGE OUR FINDINGS, OUR METHODS, AND OUR EXCUSES. I NOW BELIEVE THAT THE REASON TEACHING IS NOT MORE VALUED IN THE ACADEMY IS BECAUSE THE WAY WE TREAT TEACHING REMOVES IT FROM THE COMMUNITY OF SCHOLARS."

— Lee Shulman, p. 6

primary virtue of the strategy is its flexibility. As indicated by the three Faculty Reports that follow here, teaching circles can serve a range of needs and purposes while advancing a larger, more general sense that teaching is an important scholarly activity, worth talking about.

FACULTY REPORT

In June of 1994, John Jameson and Ann Heiss attended an Institute on the Peer Review of Teaching, at Stanford University — the kick-off event for AAHE's project on the same topic. As the two-person faculty team from the history department at Kent State University, John and Ann took one very clear message back home with them: the need, as they put it, "to change the culture of the department, to make teaching a more collegial, collaborative venture." Teaching circles have proven a good way to get started with that goal, as John's report indicates.

SETTING A SCHOLARLY TONE: TEACHING CIRCLES IN THE HISTORY DEPARTMENT AT KENT STATE UNIVERSITY

by John Jameson, Faculty Member, Department of History, Kent State University

When we invited colleagues to attend our first departmental teaching circle, Ann and I emphasized that teaching was serious, intellectual work, and not something we can take for granted. We wanted to set a scholarly tone.

At our opening session we talked a bit about our experience at the Stanford Institute on the Peer Review of Teaching, and about our sense, resulting from that meeting, that we need to have more and better conversation about teaching, and to talk as colleagues about what good teaching is, and how we might document it. Out of this broad purpose, the group members identified topics they were interested in, and we used their suggestions in setting the agenda for subsequent teaching circle discussions.

Getting organized: schedules and attendance

We scheduled our meetings for late afternoon, alternating between slots that worked for MWF and for TTh teaching schedules. Each session lasts for an hour and a half. Importantly, we make sure there are always nice refreshments, thanks to support from the provost's office.

Not only faculty but graduate students are invited, and they've made wonderful contributions. Initially I was concerned that the presence of students would inhibit faculty discussion, but it hasn't. If anything, students have helped to raise useful controversies, and to keep us honest.

Finding a focus for our conversations

Our first real session featured two faculty well known in the department: one a wonderful lecturer and the other a wonderful discussion leader. We asked each to give a brief presentation on "what worked," and then opened things up to discussion.

In general, we have been careful to be sure that each session has an identified focus. These have included teaching portfolios, discussion-method teaching, and mentoring of new faculty — the last of which was the catalyst for plans actually to establish a mentoring program for new faculty this year.

So our talk has led to action.

We also had one session on "the changing classroom," based on the idea that a lot of history teaching is lecture based. We wanted to put new possibilities in the air related to visual and technological resources: slide libraries, laser disks, and so forth, things many of us knew very little about, and that younger faculty and graduate students teaching their own sections are now, as a consequence, beginning to adopt.

We don't simply chat; we have an agenda, a topic. It's not that we have the next two years all mapped out, but we usually have the next two or three meetings clearly in mind.

The impact and success of our teaching circles

About two-thirds of department faculty participated in our first session, and the numbers have gone up from there, to about three-quarters, including history faculty from some of Kent's regional campuses. Discussion often gets so lively we have to close the door.

Graduate student participation has been gratifying, as well. The director of the graduate program put out a strong memo to graduate students to solicit their participation, and we now have about half and half, faculty and graduate students. In fact, graduate students have now put in a request for their *own* teaching circle, which began meeting in Fall 1995. (They even invited faculty!)

The teaching circles have also brought benefit for me, personally: I'm now working on a major format change in my teaching, moving away from class "bluebook" exams, because I realized that students don't write well under those circumstances. I now have them submit drafts and revise their papers. There were a few glitches, but overall this change has worked well — even in the large survey class that has more than 150 students. Our teaching circle discussions have moved me in this direction.

Good Talk About Teaching Large Classes
At the University of Georgia, faculty, graduate students, and staff from a variety of disciplines have come together to establish the Large Class Interest Group. Since 1992, members of the group have met regularly — they meet over the noon hour the first Monday of each month — to discuss techniques and strategies they've found useful when teaching large classes. The Interest Group (they don't use the term "teaching circle") has also tried to capture the "wisdom of practice" from those discussions by producing a brochure (see Gillespie in the Resources) that has been broadly distributed on campus and beyond. Recently, an electronic listserv has extended their conversation even more broadly. (See Chapter 9 for further examples of collaboration made possible through technology.)

Changing the departmental culture

This hasn't been a department where people throw chairs at each other or anything, but our teaching circles have certainly fostered greater collegiality. They've put important teaching topics on the table and changed the way people relate to one another. The dialogue about teaching has really started.

Of course it didn't hurt that our provost, Myron Henry, was supportive of our effort; but other, larger changes across the university have bolstered our progress in the department, as well. For instance, there is now a University Teaching Council, where previously we had only a Research Council. Also, the latest AAUP contract specified that merit for faculty excellence should take into account the Boyer model and treat teaching as scholarship. Before, the major focus was research.

Additionally, we have been helped by the awareness that our local effort is part of a larger, national one, and that, through the AAHE project on the peer review of teaching, colleagues on other campuses whom we respect a lot are moving in similar directions.

FACULTY REPORT

Participants in AAHE's project on the peer review of teaching, mathematicians Charles Burnap and Miriam Leiva were persuaded of the need for an approach to teaching more collegial than the solitary practices that were the norm in their department. Toward this end, they decided to encourage an open dialogue about teaching and to empha-size the department's collective responsibility for its teaching mission. As suggested by Charles and Miriam's report, a series of departmental "teaching seminars" — a variation on the idea of teaching circles — seemed an ideal way to promote these ends.

FOSTERING COLLECTIVE RESPONSIBILITY FOR STUDENT LEARNING: TEACHING SEMINARS IN THE UNIVERSITY OF NORTH CAROLINA AT CHARLOTTE MATHEMATICS DEPARTMENT

by Charles Burnap and Miriam Leiva, Faculty Members, Department of Mathematics, University of North Carolina at Charlotte

Last year, in order to begin a departmental conversation about teaching and learning, we held teaching seminars approximately once a month. The sem-inars were open to all mathematics faculty members — approximately forty to forty-five people — and attendance ranged between ten and twenty peo-ple, depending on the topic and time of year. A core population of eight to ten individuals attended every (or almost every) seminar. As always, refresh-ments, including pizza, were served to encourage participation.

Most of our teaching seminars began with a series of questions designed to stimulate discussion on a particular teaching-related topic, which was announced in advance. However, it's important to say that once the seminar was under way, the discussion was shaped by participants' interests, and we didn't feel constrained to deal with each question on our list. As much as pos-sible, the two of us tried to act as facilitators and not as directors.

After each seminar, we distributed discussion summaries to all mathe-matics faculty members (not just those who attended the seminar).

Seminar I: a focus on the department's goals for student learning

For our first seminar, we decided to focus on common goals in the teaching of mathematics — a prerequisite to eventual discussions about what constitutes good teaching practice. The first step, that is, was trying to deter-mine what we, as a department, are trying to accomplish. We began the dia-logue by asking the following questions:

1) In what ways do you teach students how mathematicians work?

2) Teaching students to reason is a goal in mathematics instruction. What are the other goals in teaching mathematics?

3) How important is it to make connections between your courses and other courses in mathematics? In other disciplines?

4) How important is it to discuss how and why a given area of mathematics was developed?

5) How important is self-discovery for students?

6) What are your concerns about teaching?

Naturally, we weren't able to address all these questions, but we did manage to generate a preliminary list of departmental goals for students' learning. We wish to help students to:

➤ Reason mathematically.

➤ Develop logical thought and critical thinking.

➤ Become mathematics problem solvers.

➤ Understand whether the results obtained are reasonable.

➤ Make bridges to abstractions.

➤ Recognize key mathematical concepts and skills.

➤ Distinguish between routine problems and those requiring creativity.

➤ Know and use mathematical language and procedures.

➤ Be able to communicate mathematically.

➤ Apply mathematical skills and knowledge in other subject areas, especially within the student's own discipline.

Seminars II and III: a focus on achieving our goals for student learning

For the next teaching seminar, we decided to focus on strategies that would help us implement the goals determined during the previous seminar. We began the discussion with two broad questions:

1) What are your concerns about teaching?

2) What specific suggestions/ideas/strategies do you have that may help us with our teaching?

The ensuing discussion was highly productive — if not always clearly focused on the goals. In the second seminar, the group talked about ways of encouraging student involvement, the formation of student study groups, and strategies for dealing with discipline problems such as students' talking during class, arriving late, and/or leaving early.

The third seminar also centered on achieving our goals, and we used the same two prompt questions. By this time, topics for discussion seemed to arise naturally. We even got into issues related to assessment, which many faculty identified as "a concern." We decided, then, to take assessment as the core topic for our fourth seminar.

Seminar IV: a focus on assessing student learning

Once again we posed a series of questions to guide the seminar discussion:

1) What we assess and how we assess it communicates what we value. A good assessment instrument should emphasize the mathematics that is most important for students to learn. What points should be emphasized?

2) Mathematics instruction and assessment should be linked so that each one reinforces the other. How can we use assessment to enhance our instruction?

3) Assessment should provide an opportunity for students to evaluate and improve their work. Does our assessment process actually result in improved performance?

4) Assessment should allow students to further their learning. Is it important to include nonroutine/open-ended problems on tests?

5) The validity of assessment is a characteristic not of the instrument itself but rather of the inferences made on the basis of the assessment. What can we learn from tests, quizzes, and homework problems?

6) Valid inferences are based on multiple sources of evidence. What methods can we use to evaluate student work?

Outcomes and benefits of our teaching seminars

Comments from participants indicate that the teaching seminars were helpful to many individuals in the department, especially those who attended regularly. In general, there was a sense that the seminars fostered more conversation about teaching. One person noted, "It was useful to exchange ideas on teaching philosophy and practices. While we might not all agree on every detail, it is important to have this type of discussion." Another said, "This was a real eye-opener. I realized we were a *group* of mathematicians, but that we don't usually cooperate on our teaching efforts."

The impact of the seminars on departmental culture is harder to know, but one outcome is that there is now a core of a dozen or so individuals (out of a department of forty to forty-five) who want to continue the discussion about learning goals and teaching practices. Additionally, at the request of several graduate students, we have now begun a series of teaching seminars designed to help our teaching assistants.

Plans for a next stage of work

We will continue to promote a dialogue about teaching within our department, but many participants in the seminars feel that it is now time to channel our efforts into discussions directed toward specific courses or groups of courses. As a starting point for these discussions, we could use the course files that we have established [see Burnap's Faculty Report in Chapter 8]. We could also try to take advantage of some existing administrative structures: The department has recently established a Calculus Sequence Committee (charged with overseeing our implementation of reformed calculus material) and a Differential Equations Committee (charged with overseeing an introductory differential equations course).

Looking back, we are pleased with the seminars strategy. We considered other options for departmental action but felt that we could best build faculty involvement by taking advantage of the extensive discussion of teaching goals and practices within the mathematics education literature. By drawing on this material we provided a framework that was also an icebreaker.

A Focus on First-Year Students at Alverno College

At Alverno College, a group of faculty who teach first-year students has met, brown-bag-lunch-style, once a week, for a dozen years now. The agenda for their discussions is fairly open, says long-time participant Timothy Riordan, professor of philosophy; typically, one person agrees to get the conversation started on a topic determined by the group the previous week. Not everyone comes every time, of course, but, in the spirit of teaching circles, the conversation has a sustained, evolving quality. It's an opportunity, Tim says, "to learn more about the experiences students are having *across* their courses, and to think together about helping them have a more integrated, connected experience in their first year."

In this example, technology is both the subject of and the primary vehicle for good conversation about teaching and learning. In response to a new learning resource on campus — access for students to an "On-Line Forum" offered in conjunction with a number of courses — faculty teaching those courses have constituted what is, in effect, their own (mostly) online teaching circle, aimed at learning from one another how to assist students to use the Forum. Susan Obler, the group's facilitator, describes how new technologies have contributed to faculty — and student — conversation about teaching and learning.

LEARNING TOGETHER: AN ONLINE FACULTY CONVERSATION ABOUT ONLINE STUDENT CONVERSATION AT RIO HONDO COLLEGE

by Susan Obler, Director, Teaching and Learning Center, Rio Hondo College

Like lots of campuses these days, Rio Hondo has been working to integrate new instructional technologies into its courses — one of those being a new On-Line Forum offered in conjunction with a number of courses. What the Forum has meant for our very diverse student body is a new way of being "involved." The traditional image of involvement is speaking aloud in class, but for many of our students, that's simply not a part of their culture. Now, given an alternative mode through the On-Line Forum, they just shine.

A faculty need for mutual assistance

Meanwhile, of course, the faculty, most of whom have limited experience with these kinds of things themselves, are trying to figure out how to manage and make the most of this new mode of student involvement and communication. Our goal is to use the Forum to foster higher-order thinking, and to help students develop "a voice" and a sense of personal authority. Unfortunately, faculty have found that much of the students' online conversation has a "talk-show" or sound-bite quality to it, which doesn't foster these learning goals.

In short, the On-Line Forum has been a kind of "oops" experience for faculty, and a group of them is now meeting (under the auspices of a Title III grant) to try to sort out a variety of issues, ranging from the epistemological (how knowledge is constructed in these kinds of conversations, and what kinds of prompts yield the most constructive conversations) to the practical (how to help students deal with flaming, or how to simplify the logon procedure).

The composition of the group

The faculty group is highly interdisciplinary, including folks teaching courses in psychology, economics, astronomy, history of minorities, child development, British literature, English composition, U.S. history, career exploration, and Internet research (each of which has an associated On-Line Forum). Mostly, and appropriately, these faculty "meet" electronically, on their *own* online forum, but we also get together in person occasionally. Much of the talk, whether face-to-face or electronic — is about purposes:

what kinds of conversations we want to see students having online, and how those conversations can be fostered and facilitated.

A collective task: doing assessment together

At our last gathering, we decided to do a collaborative classroom assessment at the end of the semester, with everyone agreeing to ask students to respond anonymously to the question: In what ways has the On-Line Forum supported learning in this class?

We have just completed this assessment, with students telling us that the Forum helps them (1) see a range of views on topics we deal with in class; (2) understand other cultures; and (3) practice with technologies that they need in the world of work. This feedback will now be grist for a next stage of faculty conversation.

(For a copy of the project report and curriculum materials for the On-Line Forum, contact Susan Obler at: <obler@www.rh.cc.ca.us>.)

ADAPTING TEACHING CIRCLES TO DIFFERENT DISCIPLINES

John Jameson's report above focuses on the use of teaching circles in the history department at Kent State University, but in fact the institution has used the same strategy in three additional departments, whose experiences suggest how the model might be adapted to suit different disciplinary cultures and interests.

In Kent's English department, for instance, the teaching circle is organized around a single course — the Freshman Honors Colloquium. Bringing the instructors of that multi-section course together several times a semester was, says Larry Andrews (who heads up the group and is dean of the Honors College) "a natural," for a large department "where we never seem to get together in common-interest groups."

In nursing, teaching circles have taken a more task-force-like form, more formal and highly focused than in the other departments, and more in keeping with the department's habit of working collectively on all kinds of agendas.

In math, teaching circles have been shaped to parallel an existing series of research colloquia, giving them a familiar feel and a more "disciplined" quality. (As a mathematician on another campus that has employed teaching circles told me, "mathematicians are allergic to anything with a touchy-feely quality," which some might see in the term "teaching circles.")

SUGGESTIONS FOR CONDUCTING EFFECTIVE TEACHING CIRCLES

Regardless of the departmental context, and whatever the specific focus of the teaching circle, three basic principles are likely to make the strategy more productive:

1) Be clear about the purpose of the group: What is it that participants want from the experience? An important first discussion should be about goals, expectations, and ground rules.

2) Keep discussions focused on concrete particulars — for instance, by sharing syllabi or samples of student work, or by visiting one another's class-

es. General discussions of teaching are likely to be less useful than those that focus on the specifics of "our students and our curriculum."

3) Think about how to preserve and share the work of the teaching circle — be it through a set of minutes following each session (as in the example above from UNC at Charlotte), a publication (such as the brochure produced by the Large Class Interest Group at the University of Georgia), a "collective course portfolio," or some other product.

RESOURCES

Bernstein, Daniel J. "A Departmental System for Balancing the Development and Evaluation of College Teaching: A Commentary on Cavanagh." *Innovative Higher Education* 20 (4): 241-248 (Summer 1996).

> As noted in this chapter, Bernstein coined the phrase "teaching circles" and established their use at the University of Nebraska. His article, part of a special issue of *IHE* focusing on peer collaboration and review of teaching, talks not about the mechanics of teaching circles but about their place in a larger set of departmental activities and practices, both "formative" and "summative." Bernstein describes a "longitudinal, multi-year process," which begins with promoting a climate "in which there are regularly scheduled occasions for peer conversation and interaction about teaching issues" — that is, teaching circles.

Gillespie, Frank, ed. "Teaching Large Classes." Athens, GA: University of Georgia Office of Instructional Development, 1995. Brochure.

> Compiled from suggestions generated in the Large Class Interest Group described in this chapter, this brochure lists thirteen principles for making large classes more effective, with brief accounts of strategies for implementing each. Copies are available through the University of Georgia's Office of Instructional Development, which can be reached at 706/542-1355. The Large Class Interest Group also has established an electronic discussion group. To subscribe, send the email message SUBSCRIBE LCIG YOURFIRSTNAME YOURLASTNAME to the address <LISTSERV@UGA.CC.UGA.EDU>.

McDaniel, Elizabeth A. "Faculty Collaboration for Better Teaching: Adult Learning Principles Applied to Teaching Improvement." In *To Improve the Academy: Resources for Student, Faculty, and Institutional Development,* edited by Joanne Kurfiss, pp. 94-102. Stillwater, OK: New Forums Press, 1987.

> Like several of the faculty whose work is featured in this chapter, McDaniel doesn't use the term "teaching circle," but her article deals with "tc"-like collaborations and provides a theoretical underpinning for their effective use.

Quinlan, Kathleen M. "Involving Peers in the Evaluation and Improvement of Teaching: A Menu of Strategies." *Innovative Higher Education* 20 (4): 299-308 (Summer 1996).

> Teaching circles are one of several strategies Quinlan deals with in this

article published in a special issue of *IHE* on peer collaboration and review. She draws on several of the same examples cited in this chapter.

Shulman, Lee S. "Teaching as Community Property: Putting an End to Pedagogical Solitude." *Change* 25 (6): 6-7 (November/December 1993).

Shulman argues that teaching needs to be reconnected to the work of the scholarly communities — a change that would require faculty to document their pedagogical work and to put it forward for review by their peers. Apropos of the several department-based teaching circles reported on in this chapter, Shulman contends that an important group of peers in the improvement and evaluation of teaching is faculty from one's own field: "We need to make the review, examination, and support of teaching part of the responsibility of the disciplinary community." He also talks about the pedagogical colloquium, which is featured in Chapter 8.

CHAPTER 2

RECIPROCAL VISITS AND OBSERVATIONS: OPENING THE CLASSROOM DOOR

Several years ago, I had tacked up on my office wall a quote by Oliver Goldsmith (of course I can't find it now that I want it) that went something like this: "It's hard to improve," he said, "when you have no other model than yourself to copy after." Goldsmith's point pertains to any number of human activities, but it's particularly apt when it comes to teaching, where a major obstacle to improvement is our dearth of alternative visions. We see *ourselves* in the act of teaching — or we try to — but most of us see our colleagues teach only rarely. There are obstacles to doing so, certainly: academic freedom is sometimes evoked, time is short, we may not know *how* to observe in a meaningful way. . . . But both metaphorically and literally, "opening the classroom door," through reciprocal visits and other forms of classroom observation, is an important step toward a campus culture of teaching and learning, and one with real power for faculty willing to take the risk.

This chapter features three examples of classroom observation. The first two — a pilot project at Temple University (part of the AAHE project on the peer review of teaching) and an established program at California State University-Dominguez Hills — employ reciprocal visits of the sort used in the long-standing, much-studied New Jersey Master Faculty Program (now called "Partners in Learning"), which entails (1) pairs of faculty (2) working as a team for an extended period of time (3) conducting reciprocal visits to each other's classes, (4) complemented by interviews with each other's students, and (5) all done in the context of ongoing consultation and conversation about what's happening, why, and how it could be improved. The third is from Eastern Michigan University and combines a number of elements in a (to me) new way.

What all three show is that while classroom observation focuses on only one facet of teaching — what actually goes on in the classroom — it is also a strategy with special power: (1) to prompt concrete, substantive discussion of teaching and learning, (2) to create an occasion for reflection and self-assessment, (3) and to foster colleagueship and community among faculty.

What you'll also find in this chapter are suggestions for conducting effective classroom visits, a brief discussion of videotaping (an alternative to being there?), and resources for further work.

"'OPENING THE CLASSROOM DOOR' HAS BECOME A RALLYING CRY FOR THOSE WHO WISH TO PROMOTE A TEACHING CULTURE IN HIGHER EDUCATION. ON ONE LEVEL IT IS PURELY METAPHORICAL, A SYMBOL OF THE NEED FOR OPEN DISCUSSION ABOUT WHAT WE TEACH, WHY, AND HOW. IT IS ALSO EMBLEMATIC OF THE DESIRE TO OVERCOME THE ISOLATION THAT TOO OFTEN PERVADES LIFE IN THE ACADEMY, REPLACING IT WITH A RENEWED SENSE OF COMMUNITY. BUT 'OPENING THE CLASSROOM DOOR' IS ALSO BEING USED ON THE LITERAL LEVEL TO DESCRIBE EFFORTS TO USE CLASSROOM VISITATIONS FOR PURPOSES OTHER THAN EVALUATION."

— Deborah DeZure, p. 27

William Cutler and his history department colleague Howard Spodek are participants in AAHE's peer review of teaching project. Here, Bill and then Howard describe and comment on the value of the reciprocal visits to the other's classes made in conjunction with several "exercises" undertaken by project participants in advance of an Institute on the Peer Review of Teaching, at Stanford University in the summer of 1994.

RECIPROCAL CLASSROOM VISITS: AN EXPERIMENT IN THE TEMPLE UNIVERSITY HISTORY DEPARTMENT

by William Cutler, Faculty Member, Department of History, Temple University

Howard and I had a profitable exchange when we were doing the exercises in advance of the Stanford meeting in 1994. One of the things that I enjoyed most was the informal conversation that we had before and (mainly) after visiting each other's classes where we talked about how, respectively, we approach the issue of communicating with undergraduates not predisposed to be historians or to think favorably about historical thinking or writing.

Reaching today's students

Reaching such students is a problem that most of my colleagues here in the history department at Temple — I suspect it applies to other fields, as well — worry about a lot: the fact that undergraduate students are not terribly well prepared or particularly motivated. Many of them are here to get a credential more than an education. And the question is how do you reach such students? What's the key that can open their minds?

There's no simple, single answer to that question, certainly, but one part of the solution is that we all need to spend some time reflecting on what we do to get students involved. Howard's approach is perhaps a little different from mine, though we're both very student-centered, especially when we teach students who are not going to be historians or history majors and who are taking our courses because they have to and not because they want to.

Students as agents of their own learning

For me the key is insisting that students get involved right away, whether they want to or not. You have to establish the principle right away that the course is *theirs* to shape and direct, and that you won't accept anything less than their complete involvement. They have an obligation to work and contribute in a way that you can sometimes undermine by sending a message that you'll do all the work and all they have to do is sit and listen.

The usefulness of reciprocal visits and discussion

I've learned some useful strategies from participating in the peer review project, but my exchange with Howard didn't actually change anything I do in the classroom. Its usefulness was, rather, to validate our respective approaches to a difficult issue in the teaching of history — and that was valuable in itself.

A lot of my colleagues here are very experienced classroom teachers; they've been at it for twenty-five years or longer. Not surprisingly, some of them take the position that teaching is something they already know how to do, and they don't need to think about how to do it better. Under these circumstances, teaching tends to get turned into a routine, and that's not good.

My feeling is that after a while you get into a rut, and it's good to reexamine what you're doing. If you don't find a way to examine some of the strategies and approaches you've adopted, you risk communicating to students a lack of enthusiasm and commitment. So it's a good idea no matter how experienced you are, and how well things seem to be working in the classroom, to step back and examine your teaching and your students' learning. That's one of the things that Howard's and my visits and conversations together reinforced.

The value of peer exchange around teaching is not necessarily that it leads to a change on Monday morning but that it's an opportunity genuinely to examine and reflect upon your practice.

––––––––––––––

by Howard Spodek, Faculty Member, Department of History, Temple University

Bill and I visited each other's classes as part of our work on the peer review project. We both had small classes of ten to twenty students, Bill's at the graduate level, mine undergraduate. One thing that was clear was that we teach in very similar ways. That is, our personal styles are different but the overall structure and approach is quite similar, both of us using roundtable discussion.

Afterwards we talked about what we had seen in each other's classes. I didn't, as a consequence, change much of my classroom teaching style, but I did make a change in syllabus construction. (In the AAHE project, we considered syllabus construction and assessment methods as well as classroom presentation.) I put the questions for student papers into the syllabus from the beginning. I do much more with assessment through papers than through exams. Now I try to indicate from the beginning, in the syllabus, the questions that the papers will cover.

Was it worth it? Certainly the exchange was worth doing, though it's a question of how much time it takes. Doing something that's self-reflective, self-examining is always useful — unless of course it's neurotic — and sharing it with someone else is even more useful.

In 1993, faculty at California State University-Dominguez Hills initiated a peer observation program called TOPS — Teacher Observation/Peer Support — in which pairs of faculty, usually from different disciplines, conduct reciprocal visits to each other's classrooms. In addition, participants in the program meet as a group to talk about what they're learning. Kathleen McEnerney and Jamie Webb, faculty who have played a key role in shaping and running the program from its beginning, describe TOPS's origins, impact, and special features.

THE TEACHER OBSERVATION/PEER SUPPORT (TOPS) PROGRAM AT CALIFORNIA STATE UNIVERSITY-DOMINGUEZ HILLS

by Kathleen McEnerney, Faculty Member, Clinical Sciences, and Jamie L. Webb, Faculty Member, Earth Sciences, California State University-Dominguez Hills

"WE FREQUENTLY TELL OUR STUDENTS NOT TO STUDY IN ISOLATION, YET WE CONTINUE TO TEACH IN ISOLATION. TOPS HELPS DECREASE THAT ISOLATION BY PROVIDING AN INFORMAL STRUCTURE FOR DISCUSSION OF TEACHING AND PROMOTION OF COLLEGIALITY."

— a TOPS participant

Several years ago, one of us (Kathleen) was chair of the university retention, promotion, and tenure committee, a role that entailed sending out one letter after another telling candidates that they needed to give the committee some evidence of teaching effectiveness. At the same time, some departments had started doing classroom visits for purposes of evaluation, and there was a feeling that such visits might be really useful but that we didn't really know what we were doing.

Meanwhile, the campus had gotten a Title III grant (directed by Jamie), which included a faculty development component. We decided to focus that component on classroom observation because both of us wanted to learn more about it and see whether it met needs many of us as faculty were feeling.

About 20 percent of the faculty have now participated in the program, including pretty much equal numbers of tenured and untenured faculty, and of men and women. The commitment is twelve to fifteen hours a semester, which is a manageable expectation for faculty on this campus.

Choosing a model: peers, not experts

At first we thought we should go for the expert/consultant model — a small group of folks who were specially prepared to conduct visits to the rest of us who needed help. Fortunately, through the advice of people from other campuses, we were talked out of this model and decided instead on a peer-based model — one that enacts a belief that faculty can be their own best resources.

An implication of our decision to rely on peers rather than experts is that program participants are faculty who have a real interest in being more involved in one another's teaching, but who don't necessarily know how to proceed, or how to observe and give what we have come to call "reflective feedback." Accordingly, we've put a lot of energy into a training program that gives faculty a chance to practice the process of observation and feedback. In the past, we often used videotapes of ourselves teaching to give faculty a chance to practice seeing and talking about what goes on in a colleague's classroom — a kind of mini-observation. We've now moved to a live mini-lecture — the two of us take turns giving it — that includes an active learning experience. We've also begun using written cases — by Bill Welty and Rita Silverman, of Pace University, and by Barbara Millis, of the U.S. Air Force Academy — as training materials, which allows faculty to figure out, together and inductively, "what works," rather than being given a neat little checklist.

How the observation program works

The core of TOPS is reciprocal classroom visits. Faculty pair up, on a completely voluntary basis, and observe each other's teaching. Like many such programs, this one entails previsit meetings where participants talk about which aspects of their teaching they want their partner to focus on. We've found that the preobservation visit promotes reflection on faculty values and goals for both the course as a whole and for the individual class.

Afterwards, the observer composes comments based on notes taken during class, and the partners meet to discuss the class session. Both the pre- and postobservation meetings take about forty-five minutes.

But classroom observation is only one aspect of the TOPS program. We also have group meetings among the full set of participants.

Group meetings

We originally had periodic meetings of folks participating in the observation program simply in order to keep tabs on how it was going. But we had such wonderful, rich discussions — and such fun — that we decided to build the meetings into the program. What happens, we think, is that faculty learn a lot about themselves and their teaching through their reciprocal visits — and then they want to talk with others about that learning.

Interestingly, many participants report that the group meetings are the most valuable aspect of the TOPS experience. But we think there's a kind of synergy: The discussions are rich and exciting because they draw on the visits, and the visits are more productive because of the discussions.

One thing that's striking about the discussion group is that it's idea- and solution-oriented, not a gripe session. Faculty find it very helpful to discover that others have their same problems, face their same classroom issues, and can offer real assistance out of their own experiences. There's a feeling that "I'm not in this alone." An annual retreat of TOPS participants serves to reinforce this sense of community and collegiality.

Impact and results of the program

Of course we've looked at participant satisfaction, which is high. Of the many faculty who have participated in TOPS, all but a handful report that it's had positive impact on their teaching and their students' learning.

But we have also been interested in the program's impact on more institutional goals — not just individual benefits. And so we've now begun to monitor the effects of the program on the scholarship of teaching — pedagogically focused writing and public presentations — which is an aspect of faculty work that the institution is committed to and would like to see more of. We're now starting to see this kind of impact, with TOPS participants pursuing pedagogical scholarship in a variety of ways.

"THE MAJOR BENEFIT OF TOPS? SHARING TEACHING EXPERIENCES WITH COLLEAGUES, ESPECIALLY THE SMALL GROUP DISCUSSIONS; HEARING ABOUT THE TEACHING PROBLEMS OF EVEN THE MOST EXPERIENCED TEACHERS."

— a TOPS participant

"THE PROGRAM WAS BENEFICIAL BECAUSE MANY PROBLEMS OBSERVED WERE UNKNOWN TO [ME]. AS A RESULT [I] WILL HAVE AN OPPORTUNITY TO CHOOSE A TEACHING TECHNIQUE TO ADAPT TO [MY] STUDENTS."

— a TOPS participant

Creating community

An impact that's hard to measure but one we feel is really important is the creation of a genuine intellectual community among faculty.

The sad truth is that we faculty spend a lot of time making lists of things that have to be done, and madly trying to get them checked off. We're caught up in a hundred tasks. For a lot of us, TOPS has been the one thing we do that makes us feel like part of a real intellectual community. People get to know one another, and one another's ideas; they come to value one another's company and colleagueship . . . and these are people who would never otherwise have known one another.

A colleague from TOPS called me (Jamie) at home one night and wanted my reaction to something she was going to try in her class. Afterwards she admitted to feeling slightly silly for wanting to "run it by me." But I told her that's what this is all about. It's about creating a kind of community as teachers that most of us have not experienced before.

Advice to other campuses

In some ways we started TOPS out of ignorance, simply jumping in and seeing what worked. So when we do workshops on other campuses, we resist the idea that there's one right way to proceed. We tell people: Start small, certainly, but *start*. Do something, and then see what changes and adjustments are needed to make the program really effective in your particular campus setting. You can't figure it all out ahead of time.

FACULTY REPORT

A different model of classroom observation has evolved at Eastern Michigan University under the direction of Deborah DeZure, director of the Faculty Center for Instructional Excellence. Having found that faculty are eager to see one another teach but hesitant to invite themselves into a colleague's classroom, Deb provides an opportunity for faculty to register (the number of observers is capped depending on the space and dynamics of the class) to observe a designated colleague's class session and then to participate in a debriefing discussion afterwards. As indicated in Deb's report below, excerpted from her article in Academe, *both the observers and the faculty who are observed find the experience useful and reflection prompting.*

THE FEATURED FACULTY PROGRAM AT EASTERN MICHIGAN UNIVERSITY

by Deborah DeZure, Director, Faculty Center for Instructional Excellence, Eastern Michigan University

The Featured Faculty Program offers one or two faculty observations a week in a wide range of disciplines. Featured faculty are selected on the basis of high student evaluations, recommendations of deans and department heads, and their own interest and availability to participate. Faculty across campus then register for the observations and attend both the class session and a follow-up discussion with the featured faculty member about what they have observed and experienced. . . .

Benefits to classroom observers

The program works because it speaks directly to needs felt by many instructors. They want to see how other faculty negotiate the classroom terrain and how they resolve challenges similar to those they face daily. Faculty want to see models of teaching excellence they may not have had in their own training. They want to discuss teaching with colleagues whose teaching and experience they respect. And they want these discussions to focus on problem solving, rather than become reductive gripe sessions about student inadequacies. Further, faculty want to discuss teaching in a way that combines all the forces at play in a real classroom: disciplinary content, methods of teaching, students, classroom environment, and a host of others.

Finally, they want to be able to pursue this objective without having to initiate the request to observe their fellow faculty. . . .

Although observers find the class visits stimulating, most find the discussion that follows to be the most significant part of the experience. It is there that they begin to challenge and re-examine what they do as teachers. The classroom observations provide the raw data; the discussions provide the forum for transformation and integration of those data.

Benefits to the featured faculty who are visited

The featured faculty members also find the discussion to be the richest, most useful part of the experience, but beyond that, they grow from the process of self-reflection that precedes the class. As one [visited] faculty member wrote: "I'm convinced that I was the primary beneficiary. For weeks before the observation, I kept asking myself what it is that I do to promote learning. . . . I never pursued the issue with that level of interest or depth before."

SUGGESTIONS FOR CONDUCTING EFFECTIVE CLASSROOM OBSERVATIONS

From programs like those described in this chapter, and the literature on classroom observation, it's possible to draw a number of lessons about ways to make this strategy work:

➤ Conduct repeated visits, over the course of the semester. Better yet, use a team or partner approach, in which faculty pair up (or work in small groups) to visit each other's classes over the course of the academic year.

➤ Conduct visits as part of a consultation process that involves a pre-visit conference to discuss goals for the class and for the visit, and a post-visit debriefing to discuss what happened and how the class went.

➤ Combine classroom observation with other strategies that enrich the picture: interviewing students, reviewing materials, examining samples of student work. . . .

➤ Be self-conscious about the learning that can occur for the *observer* as well as the observed.

➤ Let students know what is happening and why.

➤ Think of classroom observation as an occasion for discussion of departmental expectations: Develop a departmental framework for observing teaching, and design appropriate training for those who are conducting visits.

➤ Be purposeful about who might best visit whom. Depending on your questions and purposes, you may want someone from the same field who can comment on content; alternatively, if you're experimenting with a new teaching strategy, you might want to find a colleague who has extensive experience with that strategy.

➤ Keep track of how classroom observation is working: Study and learn from your process in order to improve it.

BUT DOES IT MAKE A DIFFERENCE? THE IMPACT OF CLASSROOM OBSERVATION PROGRAMS ON STUDENTS AND THEIR LEARNING

The programs featured in this chapter have impressive track records for participant satisfaction, but what about their impact on what actually goes on in the classroom, and on student learning? That's the question that Barbara Millis set out to study several years ago in conjunction with a FIPSE project at the University of Maryland University College, where she was director of faculty development.

"Research results were not as definitive as we had hoped," Millis concedes, but a comparative study (faculty who were visited, on the one hand; those who were not visited, teaching similar courses, on the other) showed that faculty participating in the UMUC peer observation program changed in a positive direction in all eight categories on the institution's Confidential Rating of Instructors by Students (CRIS) form. Interestingly, Millis also found that greater positive changes occurred among women faculty than men (Millis and Richlin, 1994).

USING CLASSROOM OBSERVATION FOR SUMMATIVE PURPOSES?

As a source of data for "summative" evaluation, classroom observation has a problematic track record:

> The general finding is that it does *not* provide a sound method of evaluating the teacher's in-class activities. A few classroom visits by one colleague cannot be expected to produce a reliable judgment. . . . Even when the number of colleagues is increased to three, and each makes at least two visits, the reliability of resulting evaluations is so low as to make them useless. . . . A major problem is that the anonymity of the raters cannot be preserved. It is little wonder then that where colleague visitation has been tried, all ratings tend to be very high (French-Lazovik, 1975).

This is not to say that classroom observation cannot be *made* more trustworthy. As noted by Braskamp and Ory (1994), if faculty are given proper training and experience, "their ratings based on classroom observations are sufficiently reliable (that is, there is interrater consistency) and valid (that is, there is correlation of peer assessment and other measures of teaching)" (p. 97). But as suggested by the reports in this chapter, more "formative" purposes are probably the best ones for classroom observation.

VIDEOTAPE: AN ALTERNATIVE TO BEING THERE?

If classroom observation opens the classroom *door*, videotape is perhaps a *window*. The aperture is smaller, more focused; the camera can't take in "the whole" as a human observer can. But video has a long history in teaching improvement and has a number of advantages for documenting in-class aspects of teaching.

First, and very importantly, faculty may find videotaping less intrusive than having a peer physically present in the classroom. Video affords a degree of choice and control in that the teacher might have four or five class sessions taped, then choose the one he or she wants to present to colleagues — be it for purposes of discussion and feedback or for more summative review.

Most important for purposes of improvement, perhaps, videotape creates a record that allows the teacher to step back and learn from his or her own practice: "By viewing a tape of his or her class the teacher can relive the experience from a different point of view. Teachers may become aware of aspects of their own performance, the lesson, or student behavior that they did not notice during the class session because they were too involved in the actual teaching process" (Stenson, Smith, and Perry, 1983, p. 46). According to the literature, these kinds of benefits are most likely when the teacher watches his or her tape with a trained colleague who can raise topics of discussion and encourage the teacher to become reflective — and constructive — about what they see on the tape.

Video may also be a useful supplement to classroom visits, as illustrated by the experience of two participants in AAHE's project on the peer review of teaching. Mary Anne Gaffney and her partner, Jagan Krishnan, from Temple University's accounting department, conducted reciprocal visits to each other's classes, "using videotape at the same time, so that we could go back and look again, together, at what had occurred during the sessions we observed."

One issue often noted relative to the use of video (especially as an alternative to classroom observation) is that the camera is typically focused on the teacher. But, of course, the camera can also be turned the other direction, making videotape a useful and usefully *re-playable* record of classroom dynamics and *student* behaviors that most of us can, otherwise, only partially "take in" during the actual class session.

RESOURCES

Braskamp, Larry A., and John C. Ory. *Assessing Faculty Work: Enhancing Individual and Institutional Performance.* San Francisco: Jossey-Bass, 1994.

> Braskamp and Ory approach assessment as a ongoing, professional (and organizational) development process, focusing on the need for improvement-oriented feedback and support. Among the numerous strategies they describe are classroom observation and videotaping: see their Chapter 14 for a useful review of the literature on both.

DeZure, Deborah. "Opening the Classroom Door." *Academe* 79 (5): 27-28 (September/October 1993).

> The full account of the "Featured Faculty Program" at Eastern Michigan University from which DeZure's Faculty Report in this chapter is drawn.

French-Lazovik, G. *Evaluation of College Teaching: Guidelines for Summative and Formative Procedures.* Washington, DC: Association of American Colleges, 1975.

> Reviews the literature on classroom observation, concluding that it is not "a sound method of evaluating the teacher's in-class activities," with the impossibility of evaluator anonymity being the main culprit. Instead, French-Lazovik proposes a protocol for peer evaluation by committees of faculty colleagues focused on aspects of teaching and teaching materials that students are not in a position to judge. The assumed context for this protocol is summative evaluation.

Golin, Steve. "Four Arguments for Peer Collaboration & Student Interviewing: The Master Faculty Program." *AAHE Bulletin* 43 (4): 9-10 (December 1990).

> A good, quick summary of the New Jersey program that pioneered the use of reciprocal classroom visits (in combination with student interviews and reflective writing/consultation). Golin, who served as director of the program, provides both a rationale for its effectiveness and a brief step-by-step protocol. Evaluation of the program indicates that faculty make "major changes in their teaching" as a result of the program. [See also, R.E. Rice and Sandra I. Cheldelin, "The Knower and the Known: Making the Connection: An Evaluation of the New Jersey Master Faculty Program" (Princeton, NJ: Woodrow Wilson Fellowship Program, May 1989).] Golin is especially helpful in suggesting how to build on and enrich classroom observation through related activities over time.

McEnerney, Kathleen, and Jamie L. Webb. "The View From the Back of the Classroom: A Faculty Based Peer Observation Program." *Journal of Excellence in College Teaching* in press.

> Provides further information on the Teacher Observation/Peer Support (TOPS) Program described in this chapter.

Millis, Barbara J., and Barbara B. Kaplan. "Enhancing Teaching Through Peer Classroom Observations." In *Improving College Teaching,* edited by Peter Seldin, pp. 137-149. Bolton, MA: Anker Publishing, 1995.

> Proposes classroom observation as "probably the most effective" approach to the peer review of teaching when the goal is improvement. "Peer classroom observations — when conducted in a collegial, supportive context by carefully selected and well-trained faculty using a systematic model — can positively affect perceptions of teaching and learning outcomes and foster increased collegiality." Most of the article consists of a detailed account of the University of Maryland University College peer observation program and its impact on faculty. Of particu-

lar note is that the UMUC program focuses on part-time, adjunct faculty, a population often neglected in teaching-improvement efforts.

—————, and Laurie Richlin. "Three-Year Evaluation of a Peer Consultation Program: The University of Maryland University College." University of Maryland, College Park, 1994. Manuscript.

Recounts a comparative study of the effects of peer visitation/consultation on faculty effectiveness in the classroom. The context for the study is the same program featured in Millis and Kaplan, 1995.

Rhem, James. "Peers and Teaching." *National Teaching & Learning Forum* 2 (4): 9-11 (1993).

This piece features three programs that entail classroom observation in some form, including Eastern Michigan University's Featured Faculty Program and an update on the New Jersey Master Faculty Program. The third is a peer coaching program at California State University-Sacramento, which is featured in "Coaching Talk" in Chapter 3.

Stenson, Nancy, Jan Smith, and William Perry. "Facilitating Teacher Growth: An Approach to Training and Evaluation." *The MinneTESOL Journal* 3: 42-55 (Fall 1983).

Based on a study of a series of videotaped discussions of ESL classes, the authors suggest ways that videotape can be used to improve teaching, putting particular emphasis on the need for nonthreatening feedback. The importance of actively involving the teacher in his or her own development is a central theme.

Tobias, Sheila. "Peer Perspectives on Physics." *The Physics Teacher* 26 (2): 77-80 (February 1988).

Tobias describes a process she developed and employed on numerous campuses to bring faculty from diverse fields together as "proxy students" in a class session conducted by a master teacher. The process is particularly powerful in uncovering discipline-based assumptions about pedagogy.

Wiener, Harvey S. "Collaborative Learning in the Classroom: A Guide to Evaluation." *College English* 48 (1): 52-61 (January 1986).

Wiener writes out of his "frustration as formal observer of classroom teaching performances in a university-mandated system of evaluation," observing the mismatch between new collaborative approaches being tried by faculty and the "standards we had in place for the old" paradigm. By way of moving toward new standards, he proposes eight roles or tasks that collaborative learning requires of the teacher, and that evaluators might therefore use as a framework.

MENTORING: TEACHERS TEACHING OTHER TEACHERS

The power of mentoring — and its good cousins, coaching, tutoring, and other relationships in which teachers teach other teachers — is well established. Literature on the subject points to its effectiveness in promoting individual professional development, and also in creating a sense of connectedness and community. Particularly in this second capacity, mentoring is at the very heart of the idea of this volume, not so much as a separate, self-standing strategy for peer collaboration but as an aspect and consequence of other collaborative activities — including for instance the classroom observation programs featured in the previous chapter.

Interestingly, mentoring is, on the one hand, a long-standing process in academe, and, on the other, insufficiently "built in" to faculty life today. Typically, it's seen as an "add on," a personal benefit for those inclined to pursue it, something that happens for the lucky few, a function of some magical "chemistry" between individuals, maybe even a habit that was once part of the culture but has fallen out of use. . . .

Fortunately, as illustrated by the examples in this chapter, it's also a process that many campuses are now undertaking in more robust, purposeful ways, aimed mostly at new faculty, and sometimes at graduate students, but benefitting — I think most would agree — the faculty who *do* the mentoring, as well. That's one of the lessons, certainly, of the experiences reported by faculty in this chapter.

FACULTY REPORT

David Halliburton and his colleague (and former department chair) Ron Rebholz represent Stanford's English department in AAHE's peer review of teaching project. The centerpiece of the pilot activities they designed for their department is a mentoring program for new faculty, described here by David.

A NEW FACULTY MENTORING PROGRAM IN THE STANFORD ENGLISH DEPARTMENT

by David Halliburton, Faculty Member, Department of English,
Stanford University

This is the second year of a new effort at mentoring junior faculty in the English department. For as long as I've been here, we've had a system of sorts, but it was quite informal and its purpose was really evaluative. Then, just about the time we got involved in the AAHE project on peer review, we had several new faculty members coming on board — minorities and women — and it seemed like a good time to institute a more formal mentoring system and one that would be more supportive than evaluative. In general this department is a very benign, happy place, with hardly any competition. We're a happy family, basically, and very solicitous about junior people. So the idea of doing something more with mentoring was a good fit with departmental culture.

In addition, the University has a new vice provost for faculty recruitment and retention, and we got his support for this project.

The design of the new mentoring program

My idea was to have regular meetings: Once a year the mentor and mentee would meet with the chair, going over expectations for teaching, publications, career moves, etc. The mentor and junior faculty member would then meet together at least once a quarter.

To get the process started and to be a model, I volunteered to become the mentor to a new faculty member.

We started off with a luncheon in the Faculty Club, hosted by the chair, who read aloud from class visitation reports. Then we all discussed a new research project the junior faculty person was thinking about pursuing: Was it a good idea? Was it too close to the work another scholar had recently done? We finally agreed that his better bet would be to try to publish some quasi-journalistic writing he was doing, since that was near completion. We also talked about his teaching in relation to his research and his project for a second book.

Our change strategy: just do it!

There was no elaborate change strategy behind our new mentoring program. Usually the department works by committee and consensus, but in this case our chair at the time, Ron Rebholz, who is my partner in the AAHE project, thought this was such an obviously good idea that we should simply go ahead with it.

Incentives for participation

The entire program is voluntary; nobody *has* to do it. But there are some incentives and rewards. Each mentor and mentee will receive upwards of $500. So if the department had ten new faculty, and all of them had mentors, the total outlay would be $10,000.

> **"Coaching Talk"**
> Folks I've talked to who run mentoring and other kinds of peer exchange programs have thought a lot about the kinds of feedback and interactions that are most productive for participants. In the Peer Coaching program at California State University-Sacramento, for instance, the term "coaching talk" is used to underline the distinctive kind of interaction practiced between pairs of teachers who take turns serving as each other's coach.
>
> "Coaching talk" avoids judgments and evaluations — including positive ones — even when the teacher seems to want it. Thus the effective coach does not say, "That small group task you used today was really effective; I liked how you're focusing on students' analytic abilities." Such statements, say program codirectors Linda Martin and Mark Stoner, stop reflection and short-circuit the teacher's ability to engage in self-assessment and decision making.
>
> Much better are precise, analytical questions aimed at getting the teacher to describe and reflect on his or her own practice: "What kinds of outcomes do you want in this small group exercise? How do you know when students are engaged in the analysis you want, rather than only description?" The goal of "coaching talk," say Martin and Stoner, is to help the faculty member "access and try out his or her existing repertoire" of teaching options and approaches.

The other incentives are intangible. For senior faculty like myself there's a satisfaction in helping younger colleagues. It's part of being a good departmental citizen, as well.

Issues and concerns

One of the problems is that not everybody wants to participate, and sooner or later we're going to run out of mentors. We now have eight new junior faculty, and we don't know where the next mentors are going to come from. There's no system for figuring out who's going to take on this assignment.

Second, we're finding that we may need to be clearer with mentors about the need to meet. It seems obvious, but it doesn't always happen.

Lessons

Even when you've got your concept clear and you know what you want to do, getting anything done is the problem. Our local situation is peculiar, but I think that generally speaking what you need for something like this is a planning entity that has senior, respected faculty on it. People say: "Oh, *she's* on the committee: it must be okay."

FACULTY REPORT

Several years ago, in conjunction with a new general education program, Saint Olaf College put in place, with funding from The Pew Charitable Trusts, a program designed to foster more of the kind of interdisciplinarity the new general education program is built around. Faculty pairs or small groups form around particular curricular questions, which become the center of gravity for a longer-term collegial exchange (which they call "tutoring," rather than "mentoring"). Program participant and director Jonathan Hill explains how it works.

THE FACULTY TUTORIAL PROGRAM AT SAINT OLAF COLLEGE

by Jonathan Hill, Faculty Member, Department of English, Saint Olaf College

Our Faculty Tutorial Program began in 1993. It was designed to help faculty create and teach interdisciplinary courses in a new general education curriculum that stresses interdisciplinary teaching and learning.

The tutorial format

In its basic form, the tutorial entails one-on-one teaching. A faculty member wishing to acquire some area of knowledge outside his or her own area, but necessary to the teaching of an interdisciplinary course, is tutored by a colleague with the necessary expertise. Sometimes two, three, or even four faculty can be tutored in the same tutorial.

The tutorial at work

The initiative for tutorials comes from those wishing to be tutored. Tutor and tutored must be from different disciplines. There are basic guidelines as to the number of contact hours (ten) and the total hours of work (about forty) expected of a tutorial. Additionally, all tutorials are expected to result in some tangible outcome or product, which participants themselves specify: a new or revised course syllabus, an annotated bibliography, a plan for further work, and so forth. Participants receive a modest stipend and a book allowance.

What we've found is that the simple structure and minimal organizational requirements of the tutorial mean that faculty can engage in exactly what they require to learn, in a collaboration with colleagues that is focused, personalized, and pragmatic.

Illustrative tutorials

The tutorials undertaken have cut right across discipline, rank, age, and gender. A psychologist wishing to update her knowledge of chemistry for the teaching of a lab-based psychology course was tutored by a senior colleague in chemistry. A sociologist tutored two faculty, one from social work, the other from education, in minority cultures. In preparation for a new general education requirement in Ethical Issues and Normative Perspectives, a series of tutorials on ethics was offered to a range of faculty by a philosopher. Three faculty, from chemistry, political science, and mathematics, respectively, were tutored by a colleague from English on integrating women's studies into their courses. And the list goes on.

The results

In all, over a two-and-a-half-year period, some seventy faculty have participated in forty tutorials. As measured by the program's original intention — to create interdisciplinary courses for the new GE curriculum — the harvest has yet to be fully gathered. The new curriculum is still growing, and it takes time for faculty to fit new courses into the GE curriculum while meeting their other teaching obligations.

However, reports from participants, and from outside evaluators, suggest that the program has already produced significant, if less quantifiable, benefits — personal, professional, and curricular. Tutorials, one faculty member commented, provide "space for study," an opportunity for "fruitful conversation and collegial interchange."

For those who might be skeptical about interdisciplinary work, tutorials have been a way to get "interdisciplinarity with rigor." They produce, another participant noted, "less narrow burrowers and less dilettantish dilettantes." They can humanize and ameliorate often severe intellectual and academic disagreements, for as one participant noted, "It's harder to be ideological when face-to-face with a colleague."

Overall, our tutorial program has provided just the right amount of administrative encouragement and sanction to induce faculty to do what they so frequently desire — to talk to one another, across disciplinary lines, in a sustained and focused way on intellectual matters of substance.

Group Mentoring in the IUPUI School of Nursing

The term "mentoring" typically connotes a one-on-one relationship, but as illustrated by several of the Faculty Reports in this chapter, group mentoring (a la study groups at The College of Saint Catherine, or tutorials of three or four persons at Saint Olaf) provides an interesting alternative to one-on-one arrangements. Group mentoring can also be used to supplement what goes on in one-on-one arrangements, as it is in the School of Nursing at Indiana University Purdue University Indianapolis (IUPUI), where the faculty has designed a multi-level program that employs both one-on-one and group mentoring. New faculty may have an assigned individual mentor (the process is voluntary, based on an assessment of needs at the time of appointment), but group mentoring is also provided. Each department within the School of Nursing conducts regular faculty development opportunities to socialize new faculty, with topics based on an assessment of the needs of the departmental cohort. In addition, School-wide colloquia have been designed to assist in the socialization of new faculty. In this option, new faculty are invited to meet with seasoned faculty to discuss issues identified through a formal survey. Beginning faculty have been most eager to meet with skilled clinical teachers to discuss supervision and evaluation issues, and issues relevant to the changing health care system and its impact on student learning. They have also been concerned with the particulars of the teaching-learning process, such as how to make assignments, teaching and learning strategies to maximize the potential of the clinical experience, and the preparation of teaching and learning materials.

For more information about group mentoring of nursing faculty at IUPUI, contact Margaret Applegate (317/274-0038) or Rose Mays (317/274-4353).

David Halliburton's report from Stanford points out that an important issue in mentoring is supply: How can campuses provide mentors in sufficient numbers to meet the demand? The College of Saint Catherine, in Saint Paul, Minnesota, is reframing this question from a market issue to one of public work. Marilou Eldred recounts how this idea has translated into a program for developing senior faculty leadership for mentoring and other activities that support good teaching.

THE ISSUE OF SUPPLY: FOSTERING SENIOR FACULTY LEADERSHIP AT THE COLLEGE OF SAINT CATHERINE

by Marilou Eldred, Academic Dean, The College of Saint Catherine

Our work begins with questions about what it means to think of teaching as public work: How can the craft of teaching be understood as the charge of the whole college? What are the rewards and structures that can encourage senior faculty to take leadership in such college work?

Making teaching more public

With these questions in mind, the college has for several years now sought to make teaching "more public." Faculty have created extensive interaction across different disciplines and as a whole college through interdisciplinary faculty study groups, a new core curriculum, and regular public discussions about the nature and purpose of teaching and learning.

This public culture of teaching creates the conditions for motivating senior faculty to take leadership roles in coaching younger faculty members.

The faculty resource team

Supported by a grant from The Bush Foundation, a group of senior faculty recognized for their teaching abilities — the "Faculty Resource Team" — created a mentoring program for faculty new to the college. Initially designed as a series of workshops, the program has evolved into a more effective format — interdisciplinary faculty study groups.

These groups of seven to twelve new faculty, led by members of the Resource Team, meet regularly throughout the year to explore teaching-related issues of mutual interest. Examples are the role of teaching in the classroom, the spiritual dimension of teaching and learning, and the use of teaching portfolios. Study groups provide opportunities for socialization, as well as help support teaching efforts of new faculty.

Success

One measure of the success of the program is that at least half of the new faculty participants the first year have continued in the second year. The grant funds the study groups, provides stipends for Resource Team members, and offers resources for senior faculty to develop their coaching skills. Thus the program is aimed at leadership development of experienced as well as new faculty.

(For more information about the college's program to develop senior mentors and leaders around issues of teaching, contact Pat Vallifana or Mary Reuland, The College of Saint Catherine, 2004 Randolph Avenue, Saint Paul, MN 55105.)

RESOURCES

Erickson, G.R., and B.L. Erickson. "Improving College Teaching: An Evaluation of a Teaching Consultation Procedure." *Journal of Higher Education* 50 (5): 670-683 (September/October 1979).

> While not focused on mentoring in any strict sense of the word, this piece points to the power (and provides evidence) of faculty assisting other faculty to create long-lasting change in teaching behaviors.

Lambert, Leo M., and Stacey Lane Tice. *Preparing Graduate Students to Teach: A Guide to Programs That Improve Undergraduate Education and Develop Tomorrow's Faculty.* Washington, DC: American Association for Higher Education, 1993.

> Contains descriptions of numerous department-based programs, in a wide range of disciplines, that include mentoring components for graduate students. While the focus of the volume is primarily on the benefits to graduate students themselves, senior faculty who serve as mentors also find participation in these programs eye-opening.

Menges, Robert J. "Colleagues as Catalysts for Change in Teaching." *To Improve the Academy* 6: 83-93 (1987).

> Notes that participants in programs like those featured in this and the previous chapter "report high satisfaction, more interaction with other faculty members, increased motivation, and renewed interest in teaching" (p. 91).

Stoner, Mark. "The Peer Coaching Program at California State University, Sacramento." In *Peer Review as Peer Support: Proceedings of the California State University Peer Review Conference,* edited by Vincent J. Buck. Long Beach, CA: California State University, in press.

> Provides a fuller account of the rationale and process of the CSU-Sacramento Peer Coaching program mentioned in the box in this chapter. Note that Stoner and codirector Linda Martin have also developed a videotape about their program, with guidelines and an extended example of "coaching talk." For copies of the video, contact Mark Stoner, Department of Communication Studies, California State University-Sacramento, CA 95819-6070. Cost is $25 to cover mailing and reproduction.

Weimer, Maryellen. *Improving College Teaching.* San Francisco: Jossey-Bass, 1991.

> Weimer's very useful chapter on "Colleagues Assisting Colleagues" cov-

ers several roles faculty can play, not only as evaluators but as reviewers and — apropos of this chapter — "helpers."

Wunsch, Marie A., ed. *Mentoring Revisited: Making an Impact on Individuals and Institutions*. New Directions for Teaching and Learning, no. 57. San Francisco: Jossey-Bass, Spring 1994.

A collection of essays by various authors dealing with both organizational and adult development aspects of mentoring, broadly defined to include mentoring of students and faculty. Several chapters deal explicitly with mentoring focused on teaching. Wunsch has written extensively elsewhere about the mentoring of women and persons of color, topics also dealt with in this Jossey-Bass monograph.

CHAPTER 4

A FOCUS ON STUDENT LEARNING

In June of 1994, faculty from the twelve universities participating in AAHE's project on the peer review of teaching gathered at Stanford University to work together on campus plans and to make sure that we were all "on the same page" in our understandings of the project's aims and parameters. Early on in that meeting, a chemist from Northwestern University raised his hand with a wonderful question: "Is this," he asked, "a project about evaluating teaching or is it a project about improving student learning?"

The answer, as you might imagine, was "both," but the question raised for all of us a point that continues to be central to the project and to teaching improvement efforts more generally: the need to develop strategies for peer collaboration and review of teaching that take into account — and foster improvement in — the *results* of teaching in terms of *student learning*.

WORKING TOGETHER TO UNDERSTAND STUDENTS AND THEIR LEARNING

Putting the emphasis on students and their learning has a number of benefits. First, it gets means and ends in the right relation: It is, after all, what students learn that matters most. As folks in student outcomes assessment have come to say: Learning is the test of teaching — albeit not the only one.

Second, putting the emphasis on learning mitigates otherwise divisive debates about the "best" teaching methods, where the advocates of, say, cooperative learning line up on one side of the room and the devotees of lecture on the other, pointing fingers at each other. Shifting attention from how teachers teach to what (and how well) our students learn makes for more constructive debate and problem solving.

Finally, putting the emphasis on students and their learning makes sense because (as one hears, mostly unhappily, on many campuses today) students themselves are "different," and what used to work in the classroom simply and self-evidently now does not. In short, to meet the needs of changing student populations, faculty need to understand more — and more deeply — who their students are and how they learn.

The Faculty Reports that follow here all underline the power of collaborations aimed at deeper understandings of the student experience; in addition, they point to the ways that faculty can work together to help students themselves be more active partners in shaping their learning.

When Peter Shedd and his colleague Jere Morehead — participants in AAHE's peer review of teaching project — began thinking about how to move toward greater peer collaboration and review in their department, they wanted to sample a wide array of strategies. Their pilot project was, as Peter put it, "a real smorgasbord," with plans to videotape a class, use classroom assessment techniques, review each other's course materials, write reflective memos on their syllabi, and visit each other's classes. One thing they learned was that doing any of these things all by itself was much less helpful than doing several things in combination. Another, as Peter reports below, was that interviewing students was perhaps the most helpful of all.

INTERVIEWING EACH OTHER'S STUDENTS IN THE LEGAL STUDIES PROGRAM AT THE UNIVERSITY OF GEORGIA

by Peter Shedd, Faculty Member, Department of Insurance, Legal Studies, Real Estate, and Management Science, University of Georgia

For Jere and me, the classroom visit by itself was simply not very meaningful. Maybe that's because we had already visited each other's classrooms, or maybe because our teaching styles are quite similar, but we just didn't get a lot out of the visits per se. What got us really excited about the prospects for peer collaboration and review was combining the visits with interviews of each other's students. It was through the interviews that we got the deepest, most helpful information about our teaching and our students' learning.

The power of student interviews

The interviews gave us the ability to go beyond the kind of summary statements — the almost trite statements — that we get on the end-of-the-quarter evaluation forms. They allowed us to inquire of the students: Why are you saying this? When you say, "Professor Morehead is very professional," what do you really mean, and what impact does his professionalism have on your ability to learn? We could probe student thinking beyond a simplistic, superficial statement about "a very caring teacher." We could get at what the faculty member was *doing*.

What the interviews did for us, then, was to confirm some of our instincts, and give us some good new ideas. And while we haven't approached the process in a highly scientific way, still I think we received powerful information.

How we conducted the interviews

In keeping with the idea of peer collaboration, we interviewed *each other's* students. Jere chose to focus on his two undergraduate classes, which were quite large, so we asked the students themselves to select representatives — we suggested five — whom I then would interview. In my classes, both at the graduate level, the groups were small (thirteen and eighteen, respectively) so Jere came in and interviewed the class as a group. That seemed to work fine.

During the interviews we took notes, and afterwards we met to go over our notes and talk through our findings. We did this as soon after the interview as possible, because we felt it was important to make any appropriate modifications in our classes quickly, to show the students that we were listening.

Issues we're still thinking about

One issue concerns the selection of students to interview from a larger class. Our approach to this was to ask the students themselves to identify five people who would be interviewed, but our colleagues were critical of this process, arguing that a random selection would be preferable because students will not select truly representative peers. And that might be right.

Another issue is confidentiality. There's a concern about whether the students feel free to be fully candid, knowing that what they say will be reported back to their instructor. That may be right, too. Certainly it's true that students were more comfortable talking to their instructor's peer than to their own faculty member (we also tried interviewing our *own* classes). You can't do this all by yourself. Working with a colleague is really key.

Finally, we're aware that the students themselves were not sure whether they were supposed to be speaking for the class or for themselves. That was hard for them. It's something we need to think further about.

Impact on our teaching and curriculum

First, the interviews were powerful in communicating the students' desire for some sense of connection with the faculty member and, through the faculty member, with the institution. The interviews gave us a sense of the importance of *developing* that connection, because where there's a positive connection between the student and faculty member, there's a high level of respect on both sides, and that motivates students to try, to work harder. That's a real key to enhancing the learning environment: this mutual admiration and respect that's present when things are going well.

A Protocol for Interviewing Students
"Small Group Instructional Diagnosis (SGID), developed at the University of Washington, is an interview-based technique. An instructor invites a colleague to spend about twenty-five minutes in one class period to solicit information from students. Initially, students form into groups of four to six, select an individual to take notes, and then answer two questions: 'What helps you learn in this class?' and 'What improvements would you like, and how would you suggest they be made?' (White, 1991, p. 20).

"After ten minutes of group discussion, each group reports to the entire class two or three answers to each question. The colleague summarizes their ideas, classifying and refining them until the students reach consensus on the most salient issues. The colleague reports back to the class instructor the emergent themes, assists him or her in understanding the students' perspective, and addresses possible changes. SGID is most effective in formative evaluation whereby faculty have ownership of the collected evidence. Used this way, SGID is a good catalyst for change."

— Larry Braskamp and John Ory, p. 135

More specifically, both Jere and I got ideas about changes we could (and did) make that would improve our courses.

I learned, for instance, that an aspect of my exam policy was getting in the way of students' learning. My policy when students take an exam is that they cannot ask questions; or rather, the only questions they can ask are "Can I go to the bathroom?" or "Is this a typographical error?" I don't allow any substantive questions. Jere learned in interviewing the class that this policy was bothering quite a few of the students.

When Jere reported this finding to me, I went back to the class and explained my policy: "I understand that you are concerned about this policy," I said, "and I appreciate your concern. Let me reiterate my thinking." In fact, the policy is intended to avoid giving unfair advantage to those students who are expert at having the faculty member take the exam for them; its purpose is to put everyone on equal footing, to ensure that I don't help someone *or* mislead someone. I admit, I told the students, that I may not be able to write the perfect exam question, but they have another forum for communicating with me, by explaining their answers in writing, showing how they interpret the question. . . . This further explanation seemed reasonable to students, so the next time I teach the course I will share from the outset more of my thinking behind this policy.

So that's an example of a change made as a result of the interview. It may seem modest, but I think it's a significant improvement in the learning environment.

A second example of a change can be seen in Jere's course on International Legal Transactions. Jere has a fabulous reputation as an award-winning teacher; his students always give him very high ratings. So in my interviews I really encouraged them to make suggestions for improvement, one of which was that it would really help the material come alive if he could incorporate more current events.

Jere took this suggestion to heart, and in the spring when he taught the course again he redesigned it to be very connected to current events. And when I interviewed his students in the spring, their number-one complimentary remark was how relevant the material of the course was. One student said — and you have to understand that we struggle, sometimes, even to get them to read the book — that he felt badly if he had not read the newspaper before coming to class because he had to do that to be prepared since the course was so current-events oriented.

So that just makes the point: Without the interviews, Jere would probably not have made this change, which turned an already very good course into an even more exciting one for the students.

How the interviewing process can benefit students

Of course, we believe that the interviews allowed us to make positive changes in our courses, and that students benefitted from those changes. But in addition, we found that our students *wanted* to share their perspectives, and liked seeing that we acted upon their comments and suggestions. It gave the students a sense that they were active partners in shaping the course as it was unfolding.

A lesson about formative and summative purposes

One thing we've learned from all of this is that for faculty to work together more closely on teaching it's best to begin with developmental, improvement-oriented processes, rather than with summative reviews. On the other hand, the faculty member him- or herself should be the driving force in determining what purposes — formative or summative — the information from interviews (and other strategies) is used for.

In the case of the interviews that Jere and I did, for instance, I intuitively sensed that the information we were gathering might be helpful beyond our private conversations, so I took it upon myself to write up a memo to Jere, summarizing what I had learned from his students and what he had done with that information. Initially, I think, Jere was concerned about my formalizing the process in this way. But I told him, "Jere, this just might be of benefit to you. It's yours, you decide. No one else is going to get this."

And in fact, several months later he was nominated for a teaching award and he was able to include my memo in the dossier submitted to the selection committee. He took what was a formative memo, private between the two of us, and turned it into what could be viewed as a summative item in a public dossier. I think that's the way it should work: The faculty member is in charge.

Lessons and advice to others

1) Faculty must recognize that the only thing limiting their helpfulness to each other is their imagination. There is no formula for this. Be creative, adapt ideas from elsewhere. You may just end up inventing something that's really helpful.

2) Trust is really important. There needs to be an inherent trust relationship between the partners.

[See also Chapter 9 for a Faculty Report on long-distance student interviews done by Peter Shedd and Jere Morehead.]

FACULTY REPORT

Conceived by K. Patricia Cross, UC-Berkeley professor of education, and Thomas Angelo, director of AAHE's Assessment Forum, classroom assessment is a set of techniques that faculty can use in their own classrooms to assess whether students are learning what they're teaching; the purpose of CATS (classroom assessment techniques) is not to evaluate individual student work, or to generate educational research, but to help teachers make midcourse corrections and meet student needs as learners as effectively as possible. As indicated by Susan Nummedal's account below of work at CSU-Long Beach, CATS may be even more powerful when faculty using them work together and have a chance to compare notes about what they're learning.

CLASSROOM ASSESSMENT AS A CONTEXT FOR FACULTY CONVERSATION AND COLLABORATION AT CALIFORNIA STATE UNIVERSITY-LONG BEACH

by Susan Nummedal, Faculty Member, Department of Psychology, California State University-Long Beach

Several years ago, in the context of an accreditation self-study, the CSU-Long Beach campus began thinking about what the Western Association of Schools and Colleges (WASC, its regional accrediting agency) calls "a culture of evidence" — that is, the institution's habits and processes for studying and improving the effects on student learning of its programs and teaching.

The WASC report seemed like a great opportunity to start a conversation about assessment at a variety of levels, including the classroom. A group of faculty expressed an interest in doing that, and they met pretty regularly over the next two years. As director of the Center for Faculty Development at that time, I played the role of group facilitator and resource person, though I also brought to the group my own teaching issues and questions I was interested in exploring.

Starting with questions

The group began with a workshop on classroom assessment techniques (CATS), which I conducted. I asked everyone to formulate a question or issue about their teaching that they wanted to explore or were struggling with. The idea was to formulate it as an "assess-able question," and then to work together to select or invent classroom assessment strategies for addressing the question. This worked well for most people. Some had questions that they couldn't ever really answer, but that was okay too, since the questions themselves were really interesting and got all of us thinking.

Creating community

To be perfectly frank, I didn't have much sense of where that first workshop would lead, but when it was over the group members were very clear about one thing: They knew they wanted to come back together. So that's what we started doing, with somewhere between eight and ten folks participating over the next two years.

During the first year, we met over lunch. The second year our teaching schedules changed and so did our meeting time — to early in the morning over breakfast, which is testimony, I think, to faculty's need to be in conversation about student learning and teaching — and to "break bread" together. The group was a sort of oasis of community in what was otherwise a desert of no conversation.

What we did

It's hard to talk about the group in general. It's much more important to talk about the individual members and their different experiences.

For one thing, we were all asking very different kinds of questions. For example, one faculty member in engineering joined the group with more than a year's experience using a version of the "Muddiest Point" exercise on a weekly basis in all of his classes. He continued to do this and nothing but this; the technique was very successful for him. He was giving students an opportunity to raise questions. He prepared written responses and distributed these to all of the students at the following class session. In his view, the technique was more than an opportunity to "take the pulse" of his students and find out what they were learning. It was a way to remain "in dialogue" with them, a way for *them* to become more comfortable in interactions with him and the material. He

The Muddiest Point: A Simple But Powerful Classroom Assessment Technique

"The Muddiest Point is just about the simplest Classroom Assessment Technique imaginable. It is also remarkably efficient, since it provides a high information return for a very low investment of time and energy. The technique consists of asking students to jot down a quick response to one question: 'What was the muddiest point in _____?' The focus of the Muddiest Point assessment might be a lecture, a discussion, a homework assignment, a play, or a film.

"As its name suggests, the Muddiest Point technique provides information on what students find least clear or most confusing about a particular lesson or topic. Faculty use that feedback to discover which points are most difficult for students to learn and to guide their teaching decisions about which topics to emphasize and how much time to spend on each. In response to this CAT, learners must quickly identify what they do not understand and articulate those muddy points. Consequently, even though the technique is extremely simple to administer, responding to it requires some higher-order thinking."

— Thomas Angelo and Patricia Cross, p. 154

was not interested, really, in alternative approaches to teaching; he simply wanted his *own* way to work better.

On the other end of the continuum were folks who were asking very fundamental questions about themselves as teachers, as learners, about their values.

But what was most interesting was the way people's initial, individual questions became the occasion for more general conversation. For instance, lots of us had questions that were in some way or another about student motivation, which got us into a really good, intensive discussion about students' participation in and preparation for class.

Learning from our collective intelligence

Pat Cross has noted that in her original conception of them, classroom assessment and classroom research were techniques that faculty would employ *alone,* in the privacy of their own classrooms, to answer their own particular teaching questions. What she found, however, is that lots of faculty saw CA and CR as an opportunity or vehicle for being more public about their teaching. They wanted to share the ways they used the techniques, what they were finding out, and what they were doing as a consequence.

That was true in our group, as well. For most of the members, the group was key to developing deeper understandings. We helped one another push beyond and probe our initial "reading" of classroom assessment data, for instance. We reframed one another's questions, pointing to other ways of looking at the information and at the questions.

When the issue of student participation came up, for instance, the group began asking itself a whole set of questions about why we ask students to participate. What is the purpose of classroom participation? What outcomes do we expect? Can participation be graded? If I say 10 percent of the grade is based on participation but I have no idea how to assess it validly and reliably, what am I doing? What about the students for whom English is a second language? And, how am I creating or hampering opportunities for their participation?

That kind of conversation emerged from what appeared to be an innocent question about student participation in the class. We needed one another to get at these questions. People changed one another's minds, pushed one another to see things from other perspectives. . . .

Adapting the Muddiest Point Technique
"To strengthen the teaching in a beginning course in statistics oriented to data analysis, I tried, with the cooperation of the students, an informal feedback system. Their suggestions led to some changes in the system, culminating in a three-step sequence:

"Step A. In the final few (two to four) minutes of each lecture the students wrote brief responses to three questions: (1) What was the most important point in the lecture? (2) What was the muddiest point? (3) What would you like to hear more about?

"Step B. I collected the responses on paper provided by the students (some signed, some not). For the next class meeting, I prepared a handout that gave a frequency distribution of the answers to the questions and that cleared up some inquiries or requests.

"Step C. I tried to respond to as many of the requests as I could, some in later lectures as would have occurred naturally, some with extra handouts especially prepared, some with oral remarks in class, in addition to the remarks on the response list.

"The students were most cooperative, and some expressed considerable satisfaction with the method."

— Frederick Mosteller, p. 10

Insights and issues

Our group was cross-disciplinary, with faculty from philosophy, dance, psychology, business, engineering, and Air Force ROTC. What that meant was that we focused on cross-cutting issues that faculty find significant regardless of their field: student motivation, for instance. What it also meant was that we didn't dig deeply into questions about what it means to learn the discipline. A discipline-based CAT group would have resulted in a different conversation, which would certainly be a valuable one.

FACULTY REPORT

"Total quality management" is a term that makes many faculty bristle, but colleagues working together in the Syracuse University School of Business have developed a way to apply TQM principles in their classrooms, with the promising results reported here by Frances Zollers, a participant in AAHE's peer review of teaching project.

MAKING STUDENTS MORE ACTIVE AGENTS IN THEIR LEARNING: TQM IN THE SYRACUSE UNIVERSITY SCHOOL OF BUSINESS

by Frances Zollers, Faculty Member, Law and Public Policy, Syracuse University

The business school at Syracuse, like lots of others, is hot on the trail of total quality management. It's an article of faith in the school, and something we teach our students. In fact, the person who teaches our course in quality processes came up with an instrument that I've now used to look at the quality of my own teaching. I call it the "requirements exercise."

The "requirements exercise"

It works like this: Early in the semester you ask students — our "customers" — what their "requirements" are for: (1) you, the professor, (2) their classmates, (3) the course and material, and (this is my addition to the list) (4) themselves. The top four or five "vote getters" in each category — consensus usually develops around that number of items — become the requirements for the course.

Then, every two or three weeks during the semester, small groups of students (four to six) report back to you and the class about whether the requirements are being met. In this way, everyone gets to see how things are going, and we have a chance to make mid-course corrections if necessary.

What I've found especially valuable is that the process creates an atmosphere of give-and-take. It provides an opportunity for me to remind students that, for example, they said they wanted the course to be highly participatory, but that only five people have been participating. It gives students a chance to say that I'm not meeting a requirement. We can then negotiate about how to resolve this mismatch before it becomes a barrier to learning.

Issues and opportunities

Some students find the exercise a little odd: They've never been asked these questions. And some of my colleagues say that students can't speak meaningfully to questions about what they "require"; some think the exercise invites pandering. But I've been doing it for several semesters, and I've never had a student say something unreasonable.

As to the pandering issue, my answer is that you don't have to meet every requirement the students put forward. Sometimes the exercise is an opportunity to explain that certain expectations will *not* be met, and to explain why. A student may say, "My requirement is for this course to prepare me for the CPA exam," and I can then explain that the course is not intended to serve that purpose.

RESOURCES

Angelo, Thomas A., ed. *Classroom Research: Early Lessons From Success.* New Directions for Teaching and Learning, no. 46. San Francisco: Jossey-Bass, Summer 1991.

> Essays by faculty from diverse institutions about how classroom assessment and classroom research strategies can foster more effective teaching and learning. A final three-chapter section focuses on programs in which groups of faculty work together to employ and learn from these strategies — in the spirit of the Faculty Report by Susan Nummedal earlier in this chapter.

Angelo, Thomas A., and K. Patricia Cross. *Classroom Assessment Techniques: A Handbook for College Teachers.* 2nd ed. San Francisco: Jossey-Bass, 1993.

> A hefty but well-organized, user-friendly account of strategies that faculty can use to collect feedback from students in order to make midcourse corrections; each strategy comes with examples from a range of disciplines. A premise of most of the volume is that faculty can use CA and CR to answer their *own* questions about their *own* students' learning. But recognizing that classroom assessment and research have turned out to be "a highly social, collaborative learning experience for teachers," Angelo and Cross devote a final section, with step-by-step directions, to "departmental engagement in classroom research" (pp. 382-383). A Jossey-Bass best seller.

Barr, Robert B., and John Tagg. "From Teaching to Learning — A New Paradigm for Undergraduate Education." *Change* 27 (6): 12-25 (November/December 1995).

> A useful synthesis of much of the recent thinking about what it means to focus on learning as "a test of teaching." Barr and Tagg call for a shift from the Instruction Paradigm to the Learning Paradigm in which both faculty and students are responsible for the amount and quality of student learning. The goal: "to improve continuously the quality of learning for students individually and in the aggregate." In this sense, the Learning Paradigm also fosters *collective faculty learning* and improvement: "The Learning Paradigm envisions the institution itself as a learner — over time, it continuously learns how to produce more learning with each graduating class, each entering student" (p. 14).

Braskamp, Larry A., and John C. Ory. *Assessing Faculty Work: Enhancing Individual and Institutional Performance*. San Francisco: Jossey-Bass, 1994.

Cambridge, Barbara L. "The Paradigm Shifts: Examining Quality of Teaching Through Assessment of Student Learning." *Innovative Higher Education* 20 (4): 287-298 (Summer 1996).

> Cambridge argues that because learning is the chief goal of teaching, faculty can better assess teaching through analysis of student work. She is particularly interested in the power of involving students in this process, and describes, therefore, three practices that bring together faculty, faculty peers, and students as partners in assessing teaching and learning. Both student and teacher portfolios (see Chapter 5) play a role in what Cambridge proposes. Classroom assessment also figures prominently.

Coffman, Sara Jane. "Improving Your Teaching Through Small-Group Diagnosis." *College Teaching* 39 (2): 80-82 (Spring 1991).

> Step-by-step directions for conducting small-group interviews with students at mid-semester. Coffman's assumption is that this would be done by an instructional development staff person; but the process could, with a little preparation and practice, be employed by faculty. (For a short account of the process, see the box on p. 39 in this chapter.)

Elbow, Peter. "Making Better Use of Student Evaluations of Teachers." *Association of Departments of English Bulletin,* Spring 1992, pp. 2-8.

> A motif in several of the Faculty Reports in this chapter is the value of asking students what's working (and not) in the classroom. Elbow's piece answers common objections to doing so, and provides suggestions for making student evaluations more "trustworthy" and informative. Along the way, he also proposes a number of principles of evaluation that apply equally to student *and* peer evaluation. "We can get along with much less official, careful, high-stakes, institutional evaluation of teachers . . . if we made more use of low-stakes evaluation" (p. 4).

Katz, Joseph, and Mildred Henry. *Turning Professors Into Teachers: A New Approach to Faculty Development and Student Learning*. New York: Macmillan, 1988.

> An account of the genesis of the New Jersey Master Faculty Program (mentioned in Chapter 2). Special emphasis on the power of interviewing students — as a source of insights for faculty about their teaching *and* (as indicated by Faculty Reports in this chapter) as a powerful developmental experience for students themselves.

McKeachie, Wilbert. *Teaching Tips: Strategies, Research, and Theory for College and University Teachers*. 9th ed. Lexington, MA: D.C. Heath and Company, 1994.

> For a concise account of recent thinking about how students learn, see

his section "Learning and Cognition in the College Classroom." A good foundation for the strategies and practices featured in this chapter.

Morehead, Jere W., and Peter J. Shedd. "Student Interviews: A Vital Role in the Scholarship of Teaching." *Innovative Higher Education* 20 (4): 261-270 (Summer 1996).

Elaborates on the Faculty Report by Peter Shedd in this chapter. See also, in the same issue of *IHE,* a piece by Sheri D. Sheppard, Larry Leifer, and J. Edward Carryer (pp. 271-276) responding to Morehead and Shedd's piece and recounting a different use of student interviews to assess several dimensions of teaching effectiveness in the Stanford mechanical engineering program.

Mosteller, Frederick. "'The Muddiest Point in the Lecture' as a Feedback Device." *On Teaching and Learning: The Journal of The Harvard-Danforth Center,* 3: 10-21 (April 1989).

Mosteller's full account of the classroom assessment process summarized in the box on p. 43 in this chapter. Particularly useful is his account of how he adapted the strategy over time.

White, K.E. "Mid-Course Adjustments: Using Small Group Instructional Diagnosis to Improve Teaching and Learning." *Washington Center News* 6 (1): 20-22 (1991).

CHAPTER 5

PORTFOLIOS: PUTTING THE PIECES TOGETHER

As argued in Chapter 4, student learning is an essential part of the teaching picture — a sort of bottom line, some might say — but it is not, of course, the whole of the picture. The most accurate, revealing account of a teacher's work is one that includes not only student learning but also what the teacher does — through course design, assignment-making, examinations, and day-by-day classroom activities and lectures — to foster and develop that learning. Portfolios are a vehicle that faculty can use to put together this fuller, more integrated picture of their teaching, and to share it with colleagues.

This chapter begins with a longer-than-usual set of background remarks, about the recent interest in teaching portfolios and then about a variation on the theme (and a better idea?): the course portfolio. Its Faculty Reports also focus on the course portfolio, and how it can more effectively capture the scholarly aspects of teaching.

A SHORT HISTORY OF TEACHING PORTFOLIOS

In the past five or seven years, teaching portfolios have begun, increasingly, to catch on on campuses where faculty are looking for better ways to document their teaching. Portfolios aren't new, of course; fields such as architecture and art have used them for years. In fact, a number of campuses (The Evergreen State College, for instance) have had long experience with their use and can pass important lessons along to newcomers.

Meanwhile, important work has been going on at the K-12 level. During the mid-1980s, Lee Shulman and his Stanford colleagues conducted much of the research that led to the use of portfolios as a form of "authentic assessment" of teachers who come before the National Board of Professional Teaching Standards. Seeing the possibilities of Lee's work for higher education, in 1991 AAHE produced a monograph for faculty, entitled *The Teaching Portfolio: Capturing the Scholarship in Teaching.*

Since then, a substantial literature on portfolios has developed, workshops have been held on scores of campuses and in conference settings, and portfolios have become part of the landscape of higher education. Peter Seldin, who has studied and promoted their use, estimates that the number of institutions using portfolios (though the scale of use may be quite limited) has risen from 10 to 400 in the last few years (Seldin, 1993, p. xi).

PITFALLS AND PROMISES

By most accounts, the portfolio story has been a mixed one. Predictably, the tendency in some settings has been to stuff a lot of paper into a folder and hope for the best, with little thought to the kinds and combinations of evidence that would be most useful. A widespread, related concern is that portfolios encourage pack ratting and file padding (though my own hunch is that the stories of P&T committees confronted with overstuffed boxes of files are a function not of portfolios per se but of a lack of clarity about what evidence is wanted, and what kinds of work are most valued, with faculty sending forward everything possible "just in case"). Yet another issue in portfolio use is that, in the view of many faculty, they take too much time, both to develop and to read — an issue that begs questions, of course, about benefits.

What *are* the benefits? Most important, and almost without exception in my experience, faculty who develop portfolios report that the process itself is powerfully reflection prompting; that gathering, arranging, and writing about the "artifacts" of one's teaching (especially if the process is undertaken with others) is an occasion to take stock, ask questions, self-assess. Additionally, though issues of design and structure need further thought, it seems fair to say that portfolios have three very salutary effects:

1) Portfolios make faculty *active agents* in the process of generating and compiling evidence of teaching effectiveness; where evaluation has typically seemed like something that happens *to* faculty, this shift in roles is one that many faculty welcome.

2) Portfolios have pointed the way — though as yet imperfectly — to richer, more authentic, "situated" portrayals of what teachers know and can do, a significant step forward from exclusive reliance on student ratings.

3) Portfolios have helped make teaching "community property," offering, both in the process of development and in the final product, an occasion for collegial conversation, debate, and review.

THE COURSE PORTFOLIO: A BETTER IDEA?

Until recently, most of the interest in portfolios has been around "*teaching* portfolios." The term is used differently by different people, but in general it seems safe to say that a teaching portfolio represents a broad sampling of the faculty member's pedagogical work — in a variety of different courses, over a number of years, and so forth. In fact, this broad scope is part of the virtue of the portfolio, which is, as I have come to say, "a movie, rather than a snapshot."

Sometimes, however, what's wanted is not the full movie but a closer look at a telling scene, and for that the more narrowly conceived "*course* portfolio" may be a better idea.

CAPTURING THE INTELLECTUAL SUBSTANCE AND INTEGRITY OF TEACHING

My first encounter with the course portfolio was through the work of William Cerbin, at the University of Wisconsin-La Crosse, whose report appears below. Since then a number of faculty in the AAHE peer review of teaching project also have begun developing portfolios (one of them reports on his progress in this chapter), and a clearer image of the course portfolio is beginning to emerge.

1. A focus on the course

In contrast to the typical teaching portfolio, which covers a range of

"I WOULD PROPOSE . . . THAT IF TEACHING IS GOING TO BE COMMUNITY PROPERTY IT MUST BE MADE VISIBLE THROUGH ARTIFACTS THAT CAPTURE ITS RICHNESS AND COMPLEXITY. IN THE ABSENCE OF SUCH ARTIFACTS TEACHING IS A BIT LIKE DRY ICE; IT DISAPPEARS AT ROOM TEMPERATURE. YOU MAY PROTEST, 'BUT THAT'S SO MUCH WORK!' NOTICE THAT WE DON'T QUESTION THIS NEED TO DOCUMENT WHEN IT COMES TO MORE TRADITIONAL FORMS OF SCHOLARSHIP. WE DON'T JUDGE EACH OTHER'S RESEARCH ON THE BASIS OF CASUAL CONVERSATIONS IN THE HALL; WE SAY TO OUR COLLEAGUES, 'THAT'S A LOVELY IDEA! YOU REALLY MUST WRITE IT UP.' IT MAY, IN FACT, TAKE TWO YEARS TO WRITE IT UP. BUT WE ACCEPT THIS BECAUSE IT'S CLEAR THAT SCHOLARSHIP ENTAILS AN ARTIFACT, A PRODUCT, SOME FORM OF COMMUNITY PROPERTY THAT CAN BE SHARED, DISCUSSED, CRITIQUED, EXCHANGED, BUILT UPON. SO, IF PEDAGOGY IS TO BECOME AN IMPORTANT PART OF SCHOLARSHIP, WE HAVE TO PROVIDE IT WITH THIS SAME KIND OF DOCUMENTATION AND TRANSFORMATION."

— Lee Shulman (1993), p. 7

instructional contexts, the course portfolio focuses on the unfolding of a single course, from conception to results.

Why focus on the course? Lee Shulman observes that while most teachers can be "superbly Socratic once a month . . . the real embarrassments of pedagogy are at the level of the course: the course that just doesn't quite hang together. The course where the students can't quite figure out how what you're doing this week relates to what you're doing next week, or why a major assignment is connected to the central themes of the course. The more holistic, coherent, integrated aspect of teaching is often where we fail" (1993, speech).

Conversely, it is at the level of the course that one sees real teaching excellence. The course is a powerful unit of analysis for documenting teaching because it is within the course that knowledge of the field intersects with knowledge about particular students and their learning.

2. A special focus on student learning

When referring to course portfolios, Bill Cerbin speaks of "learning-centered evaluation," which is to say that at the heart of the course portfolio, its center of gravity, are data the teacher gathers about students' learning and development (through the use of classroom assessment techniques, interviews with students, examination of student work, etc.). The Faculty Reports below from both Cerbin and Steve Dunbar underline this key aspect of the course portfolio.

3. An analogy with a scholarly project

Many faculty are attracted to the argument made by Ernest Boyer (1990) in *Scholarship Reconsidered* that teaching should be seen as a scholarly activity. But most existing methods for documenting teaching treat teaching primarily as technique, with little attention to those aspects that make it scholarly. In contrast, the course portfolio is structured in a way that treats teaching as a kind of scholarly project.

Like a good scholarly project, a well-taught course can be characterized as having (at a minimum) three elements:

➤ it begins with significant goals and intentions;

➤ those goals and intentions are enacted or carried out in appropriate ways; and

➤ it leads to relevant results or outcomes in the form of student learning.

Moreover, it is the relationship or congruence *among* these elements that makes for effectiveness. We expect a research project to shed light on the questions and issues that shape it; we expect the methods used in carrying out the project to be congruent with the outcomes sought. And the same can be said of teaching. By encompassing and connecting all three elements — planning, implementation, and results — the course portfolio has the distinctive advantage of representing the intellectual integrity of teaching.

In 1992, William Cerbin, a psychology professor at the University of Wisconsin-La Crosse, set about to develop a variation on the teaching portfolio — a portfolio focused on a single course. In his report below, Bill explains what prompted his interest in this new genre, how he went about the process of invention and development, and with what results.

INVENTING A NEW GENRE: THE COURSE PORTFOLIO AT THE UNIVERSITY OF WISCONSIN-LA CROSSE

by William Cerbin, Faculty Member, Department of Psychology, University of Wisconsin-La Crosse

At the time I came up with the idea of developing a course portfolio, I was in my twelfth year of teaching here at La Crosse, and one of my ongoing dissatisfactions was with the evaluation of teaching. For starters, I wasn't learning anything much from student ratings anymore; I had had twelve years of those data and had, I think, learned just about everything I could from that kind of standard instrument. Second, the faculty review process seemed to have become a process of compiling a lot of stuff, putting it in a folder, and giving it to others who then made what they could of it. I found, too, that in most evaluations there wasn't much meaningful feedback — not much that could help me do a better job. And finally, the whole process seemed to have become a kind of ritual, which required a lot of time but gave little payoff. So part of my initial interest in the course portfolio came out of this whole set of concerns.

But it also came out of some new opportunities and challenges. I had recently become familiar with classroom assessment, reading Pat Cross and Tom Angelo's book, and attending workshops that Tom gave. I saw real promise in using classroom assessment techniques to examine how things were going in my class, and, as I'll explain in a bit, the course portfolio became a structure for conducting this examination in an ongoing, intellectually sustained way.

So this is the backdrop of the process of portfolio development I then undertook.

A new conception of teaching

Meanwhile, Ernest Boyer's *Scholarship Reconsidered* appeared, and I was very struck by his notion of the scholarship of teaching — and how that notion might take us beyond the old saw that teaching is based on scholarly acumen in one's field, brought to bear in the classroom. I wanted to explore what it was that's scholarly about the teaching I do.

Boyer's ideas were especially appealing because I was experiencing at this time a change in my own beliefs about teaching — starting to recognize that what I was doing in the classroom could and should be much more focused on student learning. It sounds a little grandiose, but I think I was reinventing myself as a teacher at this point, experiencing a change in myself that I didn't fully understand and wasn't completely comfortable with.

Topics like active learning and critical thinking were very much on my mind and I was experimenting with them. It began to dawn on me that what I was doing in the classroom was a kind of scholarly inquiry, and that teaching itself is a problematic endeavor where you face a multitude of dilemmas and problems, day in and day out, about how to enhance students' learning.

I was starting to see my classroom as a kind of laboratory, as Pat Cross says; I saw myself as engaged in a big messy experiment. And I saw the course portfolio as a vehicle for conducting this experiment, this inquiry, in a coherent way.

The value of focusing on the course

I was familiar with teaching portfolios and had read the AAHE monograph on the subject. But thinking about teaching as scholarly inquiry began to lead me in the direction of something I had not seen anyone else doing: a portfolio that focused on the course rather than on all of one's teaching. Being a social scientist, I began to think of each course, as I said earlier, as a kind of laboratory — not as a truly controlled experiment, of course, but as a setting in which you start out with goals for student learning, then you adopt teaching practices that you think will accomplish these, and along the way you can watch and see if your practices are helping to accomplish your goals, collecting evidence about effects and impact.

In this sense, each course is a kind of discrete entity with a beginning and an end, fairly discrete goals you're trying to accomplish, and, typically, a body of content you're trying to deal with.

So the course portfolio was a natural way to go for me, one that followed from my ideas about teaching and learning. I'm not sure I saw this immediately, but one thing I now see is that the course portfolio is really like a scholarly manuscript — not a finished publication, but a manuscript, a draft, of ongoing inquiry.

CONTENTS

— from William Cerbin's course portfolio

The design of the course portfolio

Having come to the realization that I wanted to construct a course portfolio, and working from the AAHE monograph on teaching portfolios, I sat down and sketched out for myself what my portfolio might look like. [See the boxes for the "Contents" and "Introduction" of Cerbin's course portfolio.]

For starters, I knew that I wanted to be able to clarify for my audience (though I wasn't fully sure who this would be, at first, besides myself) what I was trying to accomplish. So I started with something I called "the teaching statement," which explains the goals that I have for student learning and what I do that I think will contribute to students' progress toward those goals. This sounds straightforward, but writing the teaching statement turned out to be one of those major confrontations you sometimes have with yourself, where over a number of weeks I came up against a lot of major assumptions I have about teaching. So this aspect of the portfolio was both hard and very instructive.

Second, I knew that I wanted to include evidence of whether and how my goals were being accomplished, and I decided on two different sources of evidence: one was students' actual performance, on exams, papers, and classroom exercises; the other was information I solicited from them through classroom assessment techniques about their experience of the course and their learning.

I also began to develop the idea of portfolio "entries" focused on particular classroom experiences — an exercise involving small-group learning, for instance, or one focused on critical thinking. And these entries evolved as having certain pretty standard parts, like a journal article: a part that indicates what I wanted to accomplish; a part that reports what I did as a consequence; and a part where I reflect on what I learned from the "experiment" — recommendations to myself about what I'd do the next time around or even in the next class period.

In all of this, it's important to say, I was really flying by the seat of my pants, making it up as I went along. And in one sense it was actually pretty simple: As teachers, we regularly walk out of class musing and maybe worrying about how it went — what fizzled and why, what worked and how well. Essentially, I took this kind of rumination that most teachers do and ratcheted it up a couple steps, adding a process of evidence gathering, reflective writing, and documentation.

Impacts and consequences of the course portfolio

First, doing the portfolio helped me get a better handle on what my students were actually experiencing and learning, which was sometimes, I hasten to say, not exactly what I intended or hoped; it made me a "classroom assessment-type" of teacher: somebody who looks at teaching through the lens of student learning. And this was a very important shift. Like lots of faculty, I started out as a very traditional classroom teacher, lecturing and occupying all of the time, organizing and controlling everything that went on, telling students what to learn . . . and thinking that things were going pretty well if I covered the things I set out to cover for the day. In fact, I was getting very good evaluations from students; they were quite satisfied with the class and my teaching. By traditional measures, things

Introduction to My Course Portfolio
"I developed this portfolio to help me understand, document, assess, and enhance teaching and learning in a course I taught in fall 1992. It represents one version of what a course portfolio can look like and what it can do to enhance teaching and learning. The course portfolio is founded upon two central ideas. The first is that the primary aim of teaching is to enhance students' learning, thinking, and development. Teaching and learning are interdependent endeavors, and to me it makes no sense to examine one without examining the other. Therefore I have tried to make this a 'learning-centered' portfolio. The second idea is that a single course is an ideal context in which to explore relationships between teaching and learning. Courses represent coherent entities in which teachers integrate content and teaching practices to accomplish specific aims within a particular time period.

"A course portfolio creates a coherent view of teaching and learning throughout an entire course. It explains what the instructor intends to accomplish with students, how the teacher uses various teaching practices to address these aims, and the results of the experience in terms of students' learning, thinking, and development. Portfolios provide a way to document the substance and complexity of teaching in a course, and can be used to structure self-assessment as well as peer review. The course portfolio can also be used to document and assess students' learning and thinking, and development."

— from William Cerbin's course portfolio

were going quite smoothly. But the portfolio epitomized a different kind of teaching practice, which I had been moving toward over some years, of looking at teaching through the lens of student learning, adopting the students' perspective a lot more, and using their performance as an important measure of my success.

Second, the process of portfolio development forced me to confront inconsistencies and even downright contradictions between what I was doing in class and my stated beliefs and goals. For example, I would say that it was important for students to think critically, to be active learners; but when I actually looked at what I was doing, I realized that *I* was sometimes the one doing most of the critical thinking and active learning. So the portfolio was a kind of awakening for me — that I needed to reconcile these inconsistencies.

In some global sense, I guess I'd say that the major impact of the course portfolio is that I now understand myself better as a teacher.

Audiences for the portfolio: colleagues and students

One really wonderful experience came when I sent a draft of one of my course portfolio entries to a faculty colleague. In response, he sent me three pages of very detailed, analytical feedback. Well, this was quite a jarring experience: It was the first time I had received really pointed, albeit constructive feedback on my teaching. It's the kind of exchange we take for granted around our research, but I had not previously experienced around my teaching.

I also realized early on that students should be an audience for at least some parts of the portfolio: They were key actors in its development, and I wanted to be sure that they understood what I was doing and why. I shared the teaching statement with them, and then rewrote it and included it in a subsequent version of the syllabus. Also, periodically, I would go back to students with the results of my inquiry and reflections and ask them to help me understand what was really going on, or to solve some problem that I thought I was uncovering. So the portfolio-development process established a stronger link between me and them, creating occasions to communicate more fully about what they were experiencing and making them more active participants in shaping the class.

Bridging formative and summative purposes

Most of what I've said about the portfolio points to its benefits to me personally, for improvement and reflective practice, but I should point out that I've also used it in a formal evaluative setting. At my institution, we go through an annual review process for merit increases, and I included my portfolio in my review folder. In fact, I wrote a cover note for it, indicating that it pertained, in my view, not only to my instructional performance but to my scholarly accomplishments. The bad news is that there was no apparent response to the portfolio; there's no campus context — yet — in which it made sense or "counted" for me. The good news is that neither did it count against me, though I was extremely candid about reporting aspects of my teaching that were problematic, things that I'm working on. I simply wasn't interested in doing the kind of portfolio where you put together all the most shining examples of your work. There's nothing wrong with reporting that you're doing a really good job, of course, but my way of doing that was to show the scholarly process I engage in as a teacher, one that gets at the gaps, the questions, the problematic dimensions of teaching and learning.

Advice to others

1. There's no question but that the course portfolio takes time and energy to develop. But one of the questions I asked myself about this commitment was: How many ways can you use this thing? My experience is that the portfolio is incredibly useful to personal growth and development *and* useful, or at least potentially so, for personnel decision making.

2. You need to go into the portfolio-development process with a question or set of questions that you *really want to know the answers to*. It's the possibility of learning something that justifies the time involved.

3. Expect to be surprised by what you find out about your teaching. At a certain point I found myself nearly overwhelmed by the recognition of all the changes that I could make, or that I thought I should make. Finally, I had to say to myself: You don't have to do all of this at once. There are some student concerns that need immediate response, but other changes can be implemented over time, in subsequent courses and stages of your career.

4. Find a colleague who's willing to give you feedback. I come back to that really important experience I had in getting a colleague to respond to one of my portfolio entries. The level of exchange was way beyond the usual hallway conversation that most of us depend on. Portfolios can raise the level of discourse.

FACULTY REPORT

Course portfolios appear in a number of the pilot projects devised by departments participating in AAHE's project on the peer review of teaching. Mathematician Steve Dunbar, from the University of Nebraska-Lincoln, was particularly struck by the way the course portfolio might respond to comments by several project participants who kept "standing up during our sessions and insisting that you have to provide data about student learning if the peer review of teaching is to hold water." He was interested, as well, in using classroom assessment techniques (see Chapter 4) as a possible source of such data.

DEVELOPING A COURSE PORTFOLIO IN MATH: A REPORT FROM THE UNIVERSITY OF NEBRASKA-LINCOLN

by Steve Dunbar, Faculty Member, Department of Mathematics and Statistics, University of Nebraska-Lincoln

The portfolio I'm currently developing focuses on a course I've been teaching during the fall semester: Math 432/832, Linear Optimization, which is cross-listed as both upper-division undergraduate and beginning graduate level. It's an applied mathematics course, which means it serves the areas of management, industrial and systems engineering, and operations research, as well as math. In fact, a subtext of my portfolio is how I try to adapt the course to all these contexts while not loosing its focus as a senior-level course in my own department.

A process of setting and assessing goals for student learning

My portfolio is based on seven goals I've identified for students in the course, and my efforts to see whether I can get students to achieve them.

The first day of class, I used a classroom assessment technique that Tom Angelo calls "the background knowledge probe," asking students a series of questions related to each of the seven goals. There were four options for answering:

1) I have no idea how to solve this kind of problem.
2) I used to know how to solve this kind of problem but I forgot.
3) I could solve this if I had enough time.
4) I'm sure that I could solve this right now.

This exercise gave me "a read" on where the students started in the class with respect to the course goals. Additionally, by way of data, I've got all the homework sets, and I'm doing "minute papers" every two weeks or so — asking "What was the most meaningful thing you learned today?" and "What's still muddy?" The exams I'm giving also relate directly to goals, so that I can aggregate the results to see how well students achieve each goal.

The product

When I get done I'm going to have something fewer than fifty pages — maybe closer to thirty — that I can give to colleagues to assess — peer review — for mathematical content and validity of data: Were my goals good goals? Did I actually meet these goals?

The portfolio will be something I can give to a peer review committee that will show what I intended to accomplish, what I actually did, and what happened as a consequence; reviewers can analyze the portfolio as they would a piece of research, looking at whether the faculty member accomplished what he or she set out to do.

As I envision it, the course portfolio will not be bulky, it can be reviewed in an hour's time, and it will tell the story of the teaching of the course.

What I hope to accomplish

Partly, I just want to know whether I'm getting through to the students. And I want more than impressions about this. A statistician who recently won a Mathematics Association of America teaching award notes that they have the following saying in his field: "In God we trust, all others bring data." I want to "bring data" about my teaching effectiveness, and my students' learning, packaged in a way that will be comprehensive but easy to review. I want to show that I set good mathematical goals for the course and that my homework, tests, and projects led to these goals. Documenting the course, and knowing that others will review my documentation through the portfolio, is a way of keeping myself honest and focused.

I also want to develop the case for my own teaching. When I go up for promotion (I have tenure) I need to have some evidence of teaching excellence — the institution has made that expectation very clear — and I hope to have my portfolio put together and ready to present for review: something that will be comprehensive and data-based in a way that people haven't often seen — something the review committee can sink its teeth into.

[For more from Steve Dunbar about his course portfolio, see Shulman, Dunbar, and Sandefur, 1996.]

LESSONS FROM CAMPUS EXPERIENCE WITH PORTFOLIOS

Scores of campuses are using teaching portfolios on at least a limited scale; a number have required their use by all faculty. In general, the teaching portfolio is best thought of not as a separate, distinctive strategy for documenting teaching but as a vehicle for "putting the pieces together" in a more integrated, compelling fashion. Over the past several years, AAHE has studied campus use of teaching portfolios; a number of lessons emerge — most of which probably hold for course portfolios, as well:

1) Seek agreement at the outset about the purposes of portfolios: how the information will be used, who owns it, what's at stake. . . . Experience on many campuses to date suggests that the most powerful use of portfolios is as a tool for self-reflection and collegial sharing and discussion.

2) Be selective: The power of the portfolio comes from sampling performance, not from amassing every possible scrap of evidence.

3) Include a variety of kinds of evidence (e.g., quantitative and qualitative), from a variety of sources (e.g., former students, colleagues on another campus).

4) Provide reflective commentary on the evidence (artifacts, products of teaching, work samples, etc.) included in the portfolio. Such commentary is useful in (a) revealing the pedagogical thinking behind various kinds of evidence and artifacts; and (b) helping readers know what to look for — what the item is meant to be evidence *of*.

5) Think of the portfolio as an argument, a case, a thesis with relevant evidence and examples cited, rather than a miscellaneous collection of things. Aim for coherence around some central organizing principle(s).

6) Organize the portfolio around goals, be they your own individual goals as a teacher ("I want my students to think critically") or goals agreed upon by the department or institution.

7) Use portfolios to clarify goals, expectations, and roles. Faculty at CUNY York College, where portfolios were mandated for promotion and tenure, report that the single most important item is the "framing statement" at the beginning of the portfolio, specifying the faculty member's responsibilities, and cosigned by the department chair and faculty member.

8) Experiment with various formats and structures, be it for developing or reviewing portfolios. Be deliberate about assessing whether portfolios are "working" and how they might be refined to achieve their purposes more successfully.

RESOURCES

Anderson, Erin, ed. *Campus Use of the Teaching Portfolio.* Washington, DC: American Association for Higher Education, 1993.

Concise accounts (two to three pages each) of how twenty-five campuses are using teaching portfolios: why, on what model, with what impact, etc. Also included are sample materials (e.g., guidelines to faculty specifying what might go into the portfolio, scoring rubrics, portfolio entries . . .), along with names of contact persons on each campus.

Boyer, Ernest L. *Scholarship Reconsidered: Priorities of the Professoriate.* Princeton, NJ: Carnegie Foundation for the Advancement of Teaching, 1990.

Cerbin, William. "Connecting Assessment of Learning to Improvement of Teaching Through the Course Portfolio." *Assessment Update* 7 (1): 4-6 (January-February 1995).

Elaborates on Cerbin's report in this chapter, illustrating his concept of "learner-centered evaluation." Included is an excerpt from Cerbin's own course portfolio, focused on a classroom activity employing student groups.

Edgerton, Russell, Pat Hutchings, and Kathleen Quinlan. *The Teaching Portfolio: Capturing the Scholarship in Teaching.* Washington, DC: American Association for Higher Education, 1991.

An argument for teaching portfolios based on a conception of teaching as scholarly work for which faculty have a professional responsibility to ensure and improve quality. Based on work by Lee Shulman and his research team at Stanford, the monograph calls for portfolios organized around and designed to sample performance on "key tasks of teaching." Eight illustrative portfolio entries by faculty in a range of disciplines round out this monograph.

From Idea to Prototype: The Peer Review of Teaching: A Project Workbook, edited by Pat Hutchings. Washington, DC: American Association for Higher Education, 1995.

A collection of materials, examples, and tasks developed through a twelve-university national project on the peer review of teaching. Material behind Tab 4 focuses on the course portfolio as a way of "putting the pieces together," and provides two full portfolios: one by Eli Passow, professor of mathematics at Temple University, focused on a multi-sectioned course that fulfills a core requirement for students whose majors do not require mathematics; the other by Henry Binford, professor of history at Northwestern University, focused on the first half of a two-quarter course on the development of the modern American city.

Seldin, Peter, and Associates. *Successful Use of Teaching Portfolios.* Bolton, MA: Anker Publishing, 1993.

In this and his previous book on the subject, *The Teaching Portfolio: A Practical Guide to Improved Performance and Promotion/Tenure Decisions* (Anker, 1991), Seldin reports on his extensive work with campuses attempting to introduce teaching portfolios for various purposes.

Shulman, Lee S. "Teaching as Community Property: Putting an End to Pedagogical Solitude." *Change* 25 (6): 6-7 (November/December 1993).

> This essay is derived from Shulman's "Displaying Teaching to a Community of Peers," the plenary session address at the AAHE Conference on Faculty Roles & Rewards, San Antonio, January 1993. That speech (#93CFRR-17) is available on audiocassette from the Mobiltape Company (800/369-5718).

———— , Steven Dunbar, and Gary Sandefur. "Capturing the Scholarship in Teaching: The Course Portfolio." Presentation at the AAHE Conference on Faculty Roles & Rewards, Atlanta, January 1996.

> An audiocassette of this session (#96CFRR-63) is available from the Mobiltape Company (800/369-5718). The session also included comments by Sandefur, a sociologist at the University of Wisconsin-Madison, who is also developing a course portfolio, plus commentary by Shulman.

TEAM TEACHING AND TEACHING TEAMS

The previous chapters in this book point to the benefits of faculty talking together about teaching, visiting one another's classrooms, inquiring together into the effects of teaching on student learning, sharing work through course and teaching portfolios. . . . But as many faculty will testify, the paramount collaboration is team teaching. "Many faculty have said to me that they could go to teaching-improvement workshops until the cows come home," says Jean MacGregor in a report below on team teaching in Washington State's many "learning communities," "but teaching with colleagues is a route to 'new moves' in their teaching that they never would have learned otherwise."

Unfortunately, team teaching is an expensive arrangement as it's currently managed on most campuses, and many faculty never have the opportunity for such collaboration. Thus, this chapter features not only traditional team teaching but "teaching teams" — a term I'll use for arrangements where faculty do not actually coteach the same class but work together around multiple-section courses or linked experiences for which they have a shared responsibility. As the following Faculty Reports indicate, lots of creative possibilities exist in this regard, and they speak for themselves quite without further introduction.

FACULTY REPORT

Steve Dunbar and Mel Thornton are teammates in the AAHE project on the peer review of teaching, representing the math department at UN-L. What follows is a report, from Steve, on how colleagues teaching a newly designed calculus course developed and worked as a "teaching team," with impressive results both in terms of student success and the culture of the department.

TEACHING TEAMS IN THE MATH DEPARTMENT AT THE UNIVERSITY OF NEBRASKA-LINCOLN

by Steve Dunbar, Faculty Member, Department of Mathematics and Statistics, University of Nebraska-Lincoln

There's a ten-year-old movement in math, dating back to a conference at Tulane where the field really began to come to terms with the fact that the teaching of calculus was broken and we needed to fix it. Out of that recognition there emerged a lot of different, intertwined currents of reform — some of them technology-based, some employing cooperative learning, some focused on larger curricular reform. Now, finally, there are new textbooks on the market and lots of interesting things going on.

Our department had been watching these new developments in the teaching of calculus from the sidelines, but this last year we decided we were ready to jump into the game. It was time to make the change . . . and that change provided the context for the kind of faculty collaboration Mel and I were interested in getting started.

Forming the team

Everybody who was teaching our newly revised first-semester calculus course was part of the group. Participation wasn't actually required, though the chair was strongly encouraging it. But once things got started, people *wanted* to be there because it was useful.

The group met once a week to talk about what was going on in our classes — what was working, what wasn't. . . . We had actual formal presentations for some of the sessions — where a designated individual brought along some "artifact" from his or her section, and shared it with the group. But formal presentations turned out feeling a little stilted. So mostly we spent our time working together, hammering out what should be on the upcoming test, what the handouts should say for the third week, and so forth.

Often, one person would come with a draft of, say, a homework project, and then the rest of the group would critique it, saying this doesn't make sense, this is too vague, this is too hard, and eventually we'd get to a version that represented the collective wisdom of the group, something we were all really happy with.

Of course, what we were really talking about in large part was purpose: what we were trying to accomplish in the course.

Keys to successful collaboration

A first important context for our effort was that it coincided with a change in the curriculum — a new text, new teaching approaches. . . . This meant that everybody was in the same boat — all of us equally unfamiliar with what was going on, each one looking for help through the rough spots. That was a real key: that it wasn't the old dogs telling the new dogs what to do. There was a real, felt need to learn from and alongside one another, as peers.

Second, we had the strong support of the chair, who used a combination of arm twisting and gentle persuasion to get the group under way.

Finally, the people who were involved were among the strongest researchers we have in the department. What we did was therefore seen by everyone as respectable: If the top researchers were involved — not just the "teacher-types" — it must be okay.

Outcomes and impact of the team's work

One outcome is that the structure we started is now being woven into the departmental culture. We started with Calc I in the fall of 1994, then added Calc II and III in the spring. Those courses will continue to employ team meetings, and we're now forming a group around the fourth course in the sequence, in differential equations. Enough folks are involved that we seem to have established a kind of critical mass; we're over the threshold.

Second, we've moved from a circumstance where key courses in the department were taught on a very individualistic basis, to a much more consultative, collective model of course delivery. Previously, the only common feature of Calc I was the syllabus. We did give a common final examination, but what that often meant was that someone would wander from office to office with a draft, checking to make sure that items on the exam had actually been covered, with the consequence that the exam was gradually pared back to represent a lowest common denominator. In contrast, we now have a more negotiated, shared vision of the course, and a final exam that represents our collective high standards.

The bottom line: benefits for students

The big question for me and my colleagues is about the effect of this kind of collaboration and teamwork on the quality of the course, as measured in terms of student learning. We have two pieces of evidence about this kind of impact.

First, we have the standard student satisfaction questionnaire. Question #8 asks about overall satisfaction with the course: That went *down*. Our hunch is that this has to do with students having to work a lot harder in the new course. Also, we have a lot of students who study calculus in high school now, but in the "old-fashioned" way. Their reaction to the new course is often, "I took calculus, and this isn't calculus." So those students are often unhappy.

But a more telling statistic is the success rate: You take the third-week roster, after the initial flurry of section changing and dropping; then you figure out who from that list got a C or better. In previous semesters, the success rate in this course was about 60 percent; this time it jumped to about 75 percent.

So students didn't enjoy the course more, but they learned more.

A collective course portfolio

One of the things members of the Calc I teaching team decided to do was to write up their experiences so they were documented and could be seen by others. The result is an eighteen-page document called "Notes for Teaching Calculus at UN-L," signed by all seven group participants, and full of very concrete suggestions . . . like "When you get to this section, we found it helpful to use such and such an example"; or "Here's a good place to introduce the calculators. . . ."

There's a companion notebook that includes everyone's tests, handouts, and so forth, for the entire semester. It's a bit imposing — about an inch-and-a-half thick — but it's the kind of thing that people can look through and say, "Yes I'll borrow this item. . . . No, not that one."

What we have in these documents is a kind of collective course portfolio . . . something all the instructors signed their names to, a collaborative product of our conversations, open for public inspection. (The portfolio is available at <http://www.math.unl.edu> on the UNL Math Department homepage. Choose "Calculus Home Page," then choose "Instructor Notes." It's in TeX format, and may require TeX software at the viewing end, but most math departments will have that.)

Lessons for colleagues in other settings

A key factor for us was deciding to change the curriculum and working collectively to do it. Especially in science and math departments, that seems to be the opening wedge. We hold curriculum very dear, and when you change it you can get everyone to work collectively on it.

In 1992, Alverno College received a grant from The Pew Charitable Trusts to undertake a major reconceptualization of an integrated arts and humanities course required of all first-year students. The goal of the project, which involved faculty from the fine arts and the humanities, was to refine and update the course, but the effort also illustrates a new role for faculty in teaching one another about their respective disciplines and pedagogies. Kevin Casey, a faculty member in history and codirector of the project, describes the collaboration.

A TEAM APPROACH TO COURSE DESIGN AND TEACHING IN AN INTEGRATED ARTS AND HUMANITIES COURSE AT ALVERNO COLLEGE

by Kevin Casey, Faculty Member, Department of History, Alverno College

The course we've been working on is the first of a two-semester interdisciplinary sequence that's part of our general education curriculum. It's taught by faculty from both the Arts & Humanities and the Fine Arts divisions, which for us include eight different disciplines: history, English, religious studies, and philosophy, in A&H; and dance/movement, music, the visual arts, and theater, in Fine Arts. Although the course is not team taught, we use a common syllabus — representing our collective conception and design — and a team-designed set of class-by-class exercises, materials, and assessments.

What the team wanted to accomplish

One of the reasons that we wanted to reinvent the first course was that we had many new faculty in both divisions who hadn't been present at the creation of the course, and we felt a need to have the people currently teaching the course conceptualize — or reconceptualize — it. Another factor behind our work was that we started to notice differences in the way the faculty from the two divisions approached the arts (which are the central focus of the first-semester course). Simply put, those of us from the humanities favored a more reflective mode; our interest was primarily in examining works of arts in terms of the issues they raise, with an emphasis on formal analysis of the *product*. In contrast, the Fine Arts faculty were more interested in exploring — and having students explore — the *processes* involved in creating art. In revamping the course, we wanted to balance and integrate these two approaches more effectively.

One of our aims and struggles in trying to accomplish this integration has been to validate the different pedagogies that different disciplines can bring to the study of the arts. Our challenge was to bring forward more explicitly the issues of artistic/creative process that had gotten somewhat submerged over the years of teaching the course. And we needed to do this in a way that wouldn't be too threatening to the students: We couldn't insist they write a polished sonnet, or produce a fine piece of sculpture, but we did want to fashion experiences that would give them a sense of the artistic process that a poet or sculptor (or dancer or musician) goes through. We felt that the existing course approached the arts too much with students as consumers; we wanted students actually to experience and understand what it means to make art.

How the team worked

We have deliberately extended our work over several years, involving about twenty faculty in a variety of ways during the summer and throughout the academic year.

Our first year's work was taken up largely with conceptual questions — questions about big themes that we all cared about and might organize the course around: Why art? Why do artists make art? Why is art significant? We identified three organizing themes: art as portraiture, art as social affirmation, and art as social protest. An approach through theme worked best for us because one of the goals in the course is to help students see connections and relationships among various art forms rather than experiencing each in isolation.

With these themes in place, the first summer's design teams took responsibility for creating various parts of the course; the teams were generally interdisciplinary and cross-divisional. Each team brought its work back to the larger group for critique, then made some final revisions. By the end of the first year, we had a whole set of team-designed lesson plans, materials, assignments, and handouts. Though each of us could adapt these common materials to our own teaching approach, students had essentially the same experience regardless of whose section they were in.

At the end of each semester and in meetings of the teaching teams throughout the semester (weekly or biweekly), we discussed and kept track of what was working and what we wanted to rethink and redo . . . making a list along the way of things we wanted to revisit in the second summer. We also administered detailed student evaluations at mid-semester and at the end, which informed our ongoing revision of the course.

"WE ARE ALL, I'M SURE, AWARE OF THE MANY WAYS IN WHICH INSTITUTIONS TRY TO HELP TEACHERS IMPROVE: THROUGH MENTORING, WORKSHOPS, DEMONSTRATIONS BY 'MASTER' TEACHERS, VIDEOTAPING, AND SO ON. AGAIN FROM MY OWN EXPERIENCE IN MULTIDISCIPLINARY STUDIES, I WANT TO PUT IN A GOOD WORD FOR TEAM TEACHING. WHEN ONE PAIRS UP WITH A PEER OR WITH A SENIOR OR JUNIOR COLLEAGUE OR JOINS WITH SEVERAL FACULTY MEMBERS TO TEACH A SINGLE COURSE, IT IS ALMOST IMPOSSIBLE NOT TO BECOME MORE AWARE OF ONE'S OWN PREMISES AND HABITUAL METHODS OF PRESENTATION — NOT TO MENTION ONE'S PERSONAL MANNERISMS. ANY HINT OF DOGMATISM THAT MAY HAVE CREPT INTO A TEACHER'S EXPOSITION IS ALMOST CERTAIN TO BE CHECKED IN A TEAM, IF ONLY BECAUSE SUCH A TENDENCY WILL RUN ATHWART THE DOGMATISMS OF ANOTHER TEACHER. IN TEAM TEACHING, ONE MUST TACKLE TEXTS AND ISSUES ONE MAY NOT HAVE THOUGHT OF, OR FELT COMFORTABLE WITH, AND ALL KINDS OF HALF-BURIED ETHICAL AND POLITICAL ASSUMPTIONS ARE DRAGGED OUT FOR CRITICAL SCRUTINY. THE PROPOSITION THAT CHANGING WHAT YOU TEACH CHANGES HOW YOU TEACH IS WELL KNOWN, BUT I THINK THAT THE REVERSE IS TRUE, AS WELL, AND THAT THOSE WHO HAVE TAUGHT IN TEAMS FIND THEMSELVES RECONSIDERING THE SYLLABI EVEN OF COURSES THEY TEACH ALONE. . . . THE ONLY WAY IN WHICH ONE FACULTY MEMBER CAN OBSERVE ANOTHER UNDER NORMAL CONDITIONS IS TO TEACH IN A TEAM, AND I WOULD URGE THAT EVALUATIONS BY TEAM TEACHERS, WHICH MIGHT BE LARGELY DESCRIPTIVE, BE GIVEN A PLACE IN FACULTY REVIEWS."

— Barbara Page, pp. 17-18

Teaching each other about teaching our fields

One of the most powerful things that's happened in the process of redesigning this course is that those of us teaching the course have had opportunities to teach one another how we might teach a particular part of the course.

For example, one of the music faculty did a session for the teaching team on how he would approach the blues in this course. This meant teaching us, as "students," about the blues, but also creating a public occasion for faculty to talk about how to do that teaching — and to anticipate how our students would respond. Similarly, during the summer in-service, the dance and movement faculty actually took us through a set of dance and movement exercises that they had developed to teach students some fundamental principles of the field. So rather than just telling us how to teach it, these faculty actually took us through the process. What was unique and especially powerful was that we experienced what the students would be experiencing and had the opportunity to ask questions that we anticipated the students might ask, but also questions that we had as prospective teachers of the experience.

We have found this experiential approach to be essential in preparing faculty to teach aspects of disciplines that are very different from their own.

Costs

Faculty were compensated for participation in the summer in-services and course-design work through a grant from The Pew Charitable Trusts. Work during the regular academic year was considered part of the regular work of teaching. This approach to faculty development is very cost-effective in that it draws on the expertise that's already present in the institution.

Impact and outcomes

One consequence of our work was a better sense of what colleagues were doing in their classes, which allows us to help students make connections between, say, a history class and an art class.

But beyond this immediate benefit, we know one another better; we're better informed about one another's disciplines and how those disciplines are changing, and how the character of the discipline affects one's pedagogy. And this in turn has led to increased respect among all of us for the kinds of teaching that we aren't naturally drawn to. It's no secret that we faculty may occasionally look down on other disciplines as somehow not as rigorous or important as ours. But this collaboration has made clear why teaching takes different forms in different fields. So one big benefit is increased respect for the work that's done in other disciplines and an increased understanding of how students learn in those disciplines.

Another benefit is that many of us have expanded our pedagogical repertoire: For example, I'm now having my students do more visual kinds of work as a way of expressing their historical understandings; I'm also using historical enactments. In the past, I relied mostly on written and oral response modes, but the visual and physical-movement approaches have given me and my students more ways to express understandings. That's a product of my participation in this project.

Benefits to students

We had some students, primarily from the Art Education program, who were involved in helping to produce class materials. They also videotaped the ten-day summer in-service. This gave students who would themselves be teaching in a couple of years a wonderful window on how teachers can work together to learn about their practice. And it gave them a real sense of how much attention their faculty give to teaching, as well.

Advice to others

We found that this kind of collaboration with this many people requires a good deal of patience and time. Faculty have very different ideas and approaches to teaching, and achieving a real common ground and understanding is hard. We hit some roadblocks early in the process related to the fact that people were bringing their own, often tacit, disciplinary frameworks to bear on what the course should be . . . and we had to get these frameworks out, explicitly, on the table so they could be talked about and integrated. That took time and patience.

Second, our collaboration has asked people to teach in some fundamentally different ways. There are still some people who don't want to teach the new course. But for those of us who do teach it, the process of working as a team has made the course much more vital; certainly it's more exciting for the students. And it has raised lots of issues about how much variety we need to pursue as teachers, given the different learning styles that students bring to our courses.

FACULTY REPORT

Established in 1985, the Washington Center for Improving the Quality of Undergraduate Education works statewide, with campuses from all sectors in the state of Washington, to foster collaborative arrangements among faculty that will strengthen teaching and learning. These collaborations include several varieties of team teaching and teaching teams, known as "learning communities": "intentional curricular restructuring efforts that thematically link or cluster classes during a given term and enroll a common cohort of students" (Washington Center News, Spring 1995, p. 22). Learning communities take a variety of forms, from the more modest "linked courses" (where faculty continue to teach their own courses but in a way that's informed by others' courses), to the quite ambitious "coordinated studies" model, described below by Jean MacGregor, codirector of the Washington Center. Jean has taught in coordinated studies teams, as well as advised and debriefed dozens of faculty teaching in coordinated studies programs.

COORDINATED STUDIES: A MODEL FOR FACULTY COLLABORATION AND TEAM TEACHING IN A CONSORTIUM OF WASHINGTON CAMPUSES

by Jean MacGregor, Codirector, The Washington Center for Improving the Quality of Undergraduate Education, The Evergreen State College

In the coordinated studies model, faculty members join in partnerships of two, three, or four to team teach a course — the only course students would take in the given semester — organized around a unifying theme. The themes may be interdisciplinary (Humans and Nature in the Pacific Northwest, or Dance and Culture) or intradivisional (Molecule to Organism).

There are probably twelve campuses in Washington, including The Evergreen State College, where the idea originated, that provide this kind of offering. There's also a very long standing, similar program at the University of North Dakota, and another at Daytona Beach Community College; the newly established New Century College at George Mason University is, similarly, organizing its curriculum around the coordinated studies model. In short, coordinated studies is an idea that is growing and spreading.

Importantly, such programs serve a dual agenda of providing an alternative general education pathway for students *and* an opportunity for faculty development in which teachers "break frame," thinking about curricula and teaching in a new way.

Team teaching as faculty development

The power of this kind of team teaching around an interdisciplinary theme derives from the fact that faculty (1) leave their syllabi at the door, in order to (2) invent something entirely new with colleagues. It's this process of invention that leads to all kinds of rich conversations — about teaching and learning, of course, but also about ideas, about the disciplines and where they're going, and how each contributes to the examination of a central theme. At its best, coordinated studies is a conversation about ways of knowing — for both faculty and students.

What's interesting is that this process of collaborative invention and teaching is at once anxiety producing and very liberating. Faculty who thrive in this kind of arrangement have a strong sense of themselves as teachers of their disciplines, but they have also, typically, come to the realization that what we call Physical Anthropology, or 20th-Century Literature, or the Sociology of Deviance, is after all a construction. There *are* common agreements in the disciplines about key ideas and methods that need to be taught. But learning communities represent an opportunity to reconstruct or construct differently those key ideas and methods . . . and how to teach them.

Many faculty have said to me that they could go to teaching-improvement workshops until the cows come home, but teaching with colleagues is a route to "new moves" in their teaching that they never would have learned otherwise. One young biology teacher remarked, "You know, I went to a workshop years ago about Socratic-method teaching, but I never really 'got it' until I taught with George . . . seeing him do it, week after week. Now I use this approach regularly, and I'm excited about the *student* questioning it seems to spark."

Promoting shared responsibility

I think there's another thing that happens for faculty teaching in this kind of learning community: The act of teaching when there are both students *and* other faculty members in the classroom, all in the role of learners, is very different from having a peer *visit* your class. Your peers are present not as visitors, not as drop-in observers looking in on your teaching, but rather as co-learners and partners for the long haul. There's a quality of commitment for the whole term and the whole experience. You're in it together, working together, taking risks together, reflecting together on what's working, what might be better or different. . . .

Teaching becomes public property because it's owned by more than one person; everyone feels responsible, including the students.

Costs

One of the explanations you hear for why there isn't more of this kind of team teaching is cost. But, in fact, some of the learning community models are very low in dollar costs. Course clustering models that are team designed but not team taught do not require massive changes in FTE registrations: Let's say I teach environmental studies, and my colleague teaches a lit course; thirty students are with me at 9:00, then the same thirty go to his class at 10:00. In a more full-blown team-taught model like coordinated studies, three teachers might have the same sixty-five to seventy-five students but for the equivalent of three courses. There may have to be negotiations around space and scheduling, but real dollar costs can be managed. The bigger investment is in making the administrative arrangements for these linkages to occur, and in making time for curriculum planning, but we feel strongly that the benefits balance the costs.

Curriculum as a context for powerful collaboration

What we have found is that it is around content that faculty may feel most excited about collaborating. The best conversations begin not around a teaching method ("let's try using student groups") but around ideas that people care about. Faculty build relationships with one another less around pedagogy and more around the invention of the experience they want to give students in terms of content and ideas. Starting with content provides the necessary platform for discussion about the teaching strategies that will work best with a particular group of students.

Many coordinated studies teaching teams have picked up Evergreen's time-honored tradition of the faculty seminar, where every week for an hour or two there's time dedicated to discussing the key ideas and readings for the week. The rule is: You don't do program business; the seminar is not for talk about ordering films or designing next week's writing workshop. It's about the book we have assigned in the program this week. One of us may really know the book and has taught it, probably, but the rest of us haven't, so the opportunity to talk together about it is essential . . . and energizing!

Content is the glue in these collaborations — and the fact that we all love being learners. That's what's so compelling and delightful about teaching in a team.

About the Washington Center for Improving the Quality of Undergraduate Education

➤ Established in 1985 at The Evergreen State College as an interinstitutional consortium. The Center focuses on low-cost, high-yield approaches to educational reform, emphasizing better use and sharing of existing resources through collaboration among member institutions.

➤ Funding from the Exxon and Ford foundations established the Center; it now is supported by the Washington State Legislature.

➤ Includes forty-six participating institutions: all of the state's public four-year institutions and community colleges, two technical colleges, ten independent colleges, and one tribal college.

➤ Supports and coordinates the development of interdisciplinary "learning community" programs; approaches to math and science curricular reform; cultural pluralism initiatives; and conferences, seminars, and technical assistance on effective approaches to teaching and learning.

Established as part of Project 30, a national teacher-education reform initiative focused on integrating the arts and sciences and professional education in teacher education, the Pedagogy Seminar at Millersville University of Pennsylvania is a one-credit, optional seminar that supplements selected arts and sciences courses and is team taught by faculty in the arts and sciences and teacher education. The course was designed for students who are pursuing or exploring the possibility of a career in teaching, but it has also served participating faculty as a mechanism for self-development and ongoing curricular discussion, as described by Barbara Stengel, a faculty member in education who was instrumental in designing and implementing the Pedagogy Seminar program, for which the university received the Christa McAuliffe Showcase for Excellence award and recognition from the National Endowment for the Humanities.

TEAM TEACHING ABOUT TEACHING THE DISCIPLINES: THE PEDAGOGY SEMINAR AT MILLERSVILLE UNIVERSITY

by Barbara Stengel, Faculty Member, Department of Educational Foundations, Millersville University of Pennsylvania

"IT IS ALWAYS MY ARGUMENT . . . THAT THE REASON WE TEACH GRAMMAR IS NOT THAT WE TEACH ANYBODY ANYTHING NEW, BUT TO GIVE THEM CONSCIOUS CONTROL OVER WHAT THEY ALREADY HAVE. UNLESS YOU GET TO THAT LEVEL WHERE YOU ARE CONSCIOUSLY AWARE OF WHAT YOU ARE DOING, YOU CANNOT FULLY REAP THE BENEFITS. . . . I THINK WHAT [THE PEDAGOGY SEMINAR] FORCES THE PROFESSOR TO DO IS TO BECOME CONSCIOUSLY AWARE OF THE TECHNIQUES THAT ARE MAYBE SECOND NATURE BY THIS TIME. AND BECOMING CONSCIOUSLY AWARE, YOU MANIPULATE THEM MORE AND USE THEM MORE FULLY. I THINK IT IS A WONDERFUL OPPORTUNITY."

— Kenneth Shields, Instructor, "Transformational Grammar," and Pedagogy Seminar co-leader

The structure of the Pedagogy Seminar program is quite simple. The arts and sciences instructor conducts the primary course (e.g., in chemistry, psychology, or whatever discipline) as usual. The team member from education observes at least one session of that course each week. Then, for one hour each week — the Pedagogy Seminar — the two instructors gather with the small group of students who have chosen to participate in the seminar.

Seminars are limited to sixteen students so that they can truly be conducted as seminars, relying heavily on group interaction and discussion. The seminars are open to any students but designed especially to attract teacher-education students. Registration is strictly voluntary.

The program began in 1989; as of fall 1995, 110 of 300 Millersville faculty have participated. The range of courses included in the program is wide, including Nutrition, Ecological Biology, Transformational Grammar, The Language of Music, Physical Geology, Principles of Economics II, Modern Middle Eastern History, Modern Geometry, Sociology of the Family, and more.

The focus of the Pedagogy Seminar

The Pedagogy Seminar constitutes an exploration of a single question: How does the successful teacher transform expertise in subject matter into a form that students can comprehend? This ability, which has recently been characterized in the work of Lee Shulman as "pedagogical content knowledge," comprises four aspects: building bridges, anticipating misconceptions, representing ideas and concepts, and organizing content.

The purpose of the Pedagogy Seminar is to identify and analyze the teaching techniques employed by the primary course instructor, and to encourage students to reflect on the process of their own learning so that they will themselves be able to take course content and transform/translate it for another audience. Accordingly, the focus of the seminar is the primary course content as it is taught and learned, rather than generic principles of pedagogy.

In essence, the primary course to which the seminar is attached becomes a "case study" in pedagogical content knowledge, and the instructional team leads the seminar participants through the case.

Benefits to students

Surveys of students who have participated in the seminars reveal that more than 90 percent feel that they better understand the challenges of teaching as a result of their seminar experience. A similarly high percentage indicate that the seminar has encouraged them to be "students of teaching," closely observing the teaching techniques utilized by all their instructors.

Virtually all participants indicate that they would recommend the Pedagogy Seminar experience to other teacher-education students.

Benefits to faculty

Seminars provide a "crosscultural" conversation between arts and sciences and education faculty about issues related to teaching — establishing bonds that allow faculty to work together in teacher preparation across departmental lines.

The Pedagogy Seminars also seem to serve as vehicles for individual faculty development, enabling individuals to reflect on and, sometimes, alter their own teaching practices. In general, the Pedagogy Seminars appear to be contributing to the generation of a university that values excellence in teaching.

"TRANSFORMATIONAL GRAMMAR WAS A WHOLE NEW AREA OF LEARNING FOR ME. AND SITTING IN THE BACK OF KEN'S CLASS ALLOWED ME TO EXPERIENCE LEARNING FROM A STUDENT'S PERSPECTIVE. HOW OFTEN DO ADULTS REALLY GET TO DO THAT . . . TO THINK BACK AND REMEMBER WHAT IT WAS LIKE TO LEARN SOMETHING FOR THE FIRST TIME?"

— Mary Ann Gray, "Transformational Grammar" Pedagogy Seminar co-leader

RESOURCES

Clark, Linda, et al. *Project 30 and the Pedagogy Seminars: A Report to the Administration and Faculty.* 1991. ERIC Document No. 368 687.

> Recounts the history of the program, including its successes and obstacles faced. Transcripts of comments by faculty participants in the program (two of which are excerpted on p. 70 and p. 71 in this chapter) are lengthy but compelling.

Curricular Learning Communities Directory, compiled by Tim McLaughlin and Jean MacGregor. Olympia, WA: Washington Center for Improving the Quality of Undergraduate Education, February 1996.

> A listing of curricular restructuring efforts that link or cluster classes during a given term, often around an interdisciplinary theme, that enroll a common cohort of students. These programs represent an intentional restructuring of students' time, credit, and learning experiences, to foster more explicit intellectual connections between students, between students and their faculty, and between disciplines.

Gabelnick, Faith, Jean MacGregor, Roberta S. Matthews, and Barbara Leigh Smith. *Learning Communities: Creating Connections Among Students, Faculty, and Disciplines.* New Directions for Teaching and Learning, no. 41. San Francisco: Jossey-Bass, Spring 1990.

Places the use of learning communities in the context of twentieth-century educational theory and reform. One of its early chapters lays out five models; a final one provides extensive further resources: people, networks, and literature.

Page, Barbara. "Evaluating, Improving, and Rewarding Teaching: A Case for Collaboration." *ADE Bulletin,* no. 101, pp. 15-18 (Spring 1992).

COLLABORATIVE INQUIRY AND PEDAGOGICAL SCHOLARSHIP

In many fields today, research has become a collaborative venture. This has long been true in the sciences, but it's increasingly true in other fields, as well: Austin and Baldwin (1991) report that "collaborative scholarship has grown exponentially since World War II" (p. 3), and that "the image of the solitary scholar working alone in a library carrel or laboratory is no more than a fond memory or historical artifact" (p. 2). The same shift cannot, alas, be said to characterize teaching, where solitude continues to prevail on most campuses. But as this chapter illustrates, teaching and learning *can* be areas of powerful collaborative scholarship.

Three Faculty Reports follow here, from composition, early childhood education, and chemistry. The collaborative inquiry recounted in each begins with a local question or need — about a particular course or departmental learning goal. But all have the potential also to advance good practice more generally, through peer-reviewed scholarly publication and presentation . . . returning teaching — as Lee Shulman has urged — to the communities of conversation and evaluation that are fundamental to academic life.

FACULTY REPORT

At the University of Nebraska-Lincoln, one step in the direction of the peer review of teaching comes in the form of collaborative inquiry conducted by two faculty in the Department of English, working together to study their own theory and practice and to document their work in ways that might provide a model for others in the department seeking to "go public" with teaching. Joy Ritchie describes what she and a new colleague are doing.

COLLABORATIVE INQUIRY IN THE TEACHING OF WRITING THEORY AND PRACTICE AT THE UNIVERSITY OF NEBRASKA-LINCOLN

by Joy Ritchie, Faculty Member, Department of English, University of Nebraska-Lincoln

One thing that's working well for us is a collaboration made possible by the fact that we hired a new composition person last year. One of the courses she, Amy Goodburn, was to teach was the second semester of the first-year writing sequence — a course, I realized as coordinator of composition, we have not attended to sufficiently in recent years. Since Amy was going to be teaching this course, I asked to do so as well, seeing this as an opportunity to work with a wonderful new faculty member on an aspect of our curriculum and pedagogy what would benefit from sustained, collaborative attention.

What we did

We did some collaborative course planning before the semester started, which included writing the syllabus together; then, throughout the semester we met each week to do ongoing planning. We wanted our students to be collaborating as well, so we each had them exchange journals based on course readings with peers in the other section. Meanwhile, and in parallel with what we were asking the students to do, Amy and I kept and exchanged journals about our teaching.

People worry about the time commitment required for peer collaboration and review, but it looks more daunting than it is. What Amy and I did took about a half an hour a week, beyond our initial work on the syllabus. Usually we met face-to-face for that time, but we also used email occasionally.

A second stage of collaborative inquiry

Finding New Models for the Scholarship of Teaching

In a 1993 piece in *Change* magazine, Maryellen Weimer reviews and comments on the variety of teaching journals that now populate the academic landscape, especially those that are discipline-based (see list opposite). What she observes, with some distress, is a tendency in many of these journals to toe the traditional line in terms of methodology: "I'm struck by the fact that many of the discipline-based journals on teaching seem to model themselves on the research publications in the field — increasingly so in some instances. The applied study of teaching as it occurs in classrooms fits uncomfortably in that rigid mold" (p. 51).

What Weimer means, I take it, is that the real and pressing questions faculty face as teachers may require the invention of new genres and forms of inquiry, forms that reflect the "situated," always particular nature of teaching this subject to these students under these conditions. Narrative, cases, journals, collegial colloquies and exchanges, ethnographies, and other forms may, as illustrated by the Faculty Reports in this chapter, play a more important role in pedagogical scholarship in the future.

Our collaboration was important in a couple ways. First, it helped us develop and revise the course, which, as I say, was one of my hopes; it also led to collaboration with others who teach the course. Along the way, Amy and I developed a working relationship that we decided to extend into another semester where we saw the chance to do some collaborative inquiry around two different courses: Amy's course, a one-credit practicum on the teaching of writing (a course in pedagogical practice) and mine in composition theory. This second collaboration is intended to blur the boundary between the pedagogy and theory of the field.

Once again we're trading journals and meeting regularly to discuss issues of concern. We also each share our journal with graduate students in our course, who are, themselves, keeping teaching journals and sharing them with us and at least one of their peers. I'm using my journal as an opportunity to explore issues that are troubling or perplexing to me, particularly as related to the connection between theoretical and practical issues and changing perspectives in composition theory and practice. And what I'm uncovering is an interesting tension between the teaching model I explicitly espouse and a more traditional "delivery" model that I find myself falling back on and feeling a need for.

Another area we're exploring is generational issues, which a lot of women who teach composition have become interested in. Many of us who've been in the field longer got here by quite different, "nontraditional" routes — often (as in my case) by teaching in secondary settings or in adjunct positions. Amy and I are working from different generational perspectives in composition and rhetoric. Through writing and sharing our own histories in the field, we have located ourselves in a larger historical context and gained interesting perspectives on our theoretical positions. This, in turn, has enhanced the quality of our intergenerational collaboration and helped us explore some larger issues of professional development.

Outcomes: personal and departmental

Our work has led to collaboration this fall on two grant proposals, a new course proposal, and a proposal to do a collaborative conference presentation, which we have no doubt will result in a collaboratively written article. We see our collaboration as a model for new graduate teaching assistants, who need positive, alternative models for professional growth. We believe that our collaborative work this fall, and our emphasis on the value of collaborative teaching and research, led to a greater spirit of collaboration among graduate students. They observed one another's classes, regularly discussed their teaching, and helped one another locate resources for their seminar research projects. Two different pairs of students wrote collaborative seminar papers and are sending off proposals to turn those papers into essays for an edited collection.

But equally important, we see our collaboration as a model of peer review for the department. We will each write a letter for the other's personnel file documenting the kind of work we do. This is particularly important for Amy because she's untenured, and the chancellor has now asked that people coming up for tenure have in their dossiers evidence of teaching effectiveness.

The department has been very resistant thus far to the idea of peer reviewing teaching. But Amy and I think that one powerful way we'll present our work to our colleagues and demonstrate how peer review might work is through the promotion and tenure file that Amy will submit, which will, as a result of our collaboration, include evidence that's not otherwise typical and that will be especially compelling.

Lessons

Thinking about what we have done and what the math team has done here on this campus [both are participating in AAHE's peer review of teaching project], it seems that peer collaboration and review work very well and quite naturally in the context of course revision or development, where collaboration occurs not for its own sake but in order better to address some real problem or opportunity the department is facing.

Also, I'd note the need for a true relationship of peers, a reciprocal relationship. Of course I'm

Pedagogical Periodicals on Teaching That Cover a Family of Fields
American Society for Engineering Education (ASEE) Prism (formerly Engineering Education)
Journal of College Science Teaching
Journal of Environmental Education

Discipline-Specific Pedagogical Periodicals Where Less Than Half of the Articles Are on College Teaching
American Journal of Physics
Anthropology and Education Quarterly
Business Education Forum
College English
English Education
Journal of Health Occupations Education
Journal for Research in Mathematics Education
Journal of Architectural Education
Journal of Biological Education
Journal of Research in Music Education
Journal of Teaching in Physical Education
Physics Education
Political Science & Politics
Religious Education
Research in the Teaching of English
Teaching Statistics

Discipline-Specific Pedagogical Journals Where More Than Half of the Articles Are on College Teaching
American Biology Teacher
Biochemical Education
College Mathematics Journal
Journal of Agricultural Education (includes extension education)
Journal of Chemical Education
Journal of Health Administration Education
Journal of Marketing Education
Journal of Teaching in Physical Education
Journal of Teaching in Social Work
Journal of Teaching Writing
Mathematics and Computer Education
Mathematics Teacher
Nurse Educator
Teaching of Psychology
The History Teacher
The Journalism Educator
The Physics Teacher

Discipline-Specific Pedagogical Journals Exclusively on Postsecondary Teaching
Chemical Engineering Education
College Composition & Communication
Communication Education
Issues in Accounting Education
Journal of Accounting Education
Journal of Economic Education
Journal of Geological Education
Journal of Geography in Higher Education
Journal of Management Education (formerly Organizational Behavior Teaching Review)
Journal of Nursing Education
Journal of Social Work Education
NACTA (National Association of College Teachers of Agriculture) Journal
Teaching Philosophy
Teaching Sociology

much more senior than Amy, but we hired her because she has a lot to teach us; I saw this as an opportunity to work with her early on, and it's been great for me.

Finally, you want to be as efficient, time-wise, as possible. I mentioned above that we didn't actually spend much time on our first collaboration, and the time we did spend went to a task that needed to be done anyway. But the flip side of efficiency is effectiveness, and I would say that the multidimensional outcomes of our current, more extensive collaboration are well worth the time: What we have been doing supports our own teaching, it feeds our research in formative ways, and it also provides a model of how the department might move toward more summative kinds of peer review.

A philosophy of collaboration

We have become more strongly convinced that teaching at its best is not an isolated, solitary act. Good teaching and good theory, as bell hooks reminds us in *Teaching to Transgress,* are always collaborative. Thus, we want to emphasize that this collaboration is not something we've undertaken because it's currently fashionable; nor was it undertaken merely in the service of institutional or professional goals. Our collaboration emerges directly and intrinsically from our philosophies about teaching and research as fundamentally dialogical activities.

FACULTY REPORT

At the University of Wyoming, a three-person team is collaborating to study the effectiveness of a new method of instruction in early childhood education. Jane Nelson, a member of the team and director of the Writing Center, describes the team's aims, methods, and preliminary findings.

COLLABORATIVE INQUIRY IN AN EARLY CHILDHOOD EDUCATION COURSE AT THE UNIVERSITY OF WYOMING

by Jane Nelson, Director, Writing Center, University of Wyoming

The focus of our collaborative inquiry is a course called Observing Young Children. Peggy Cooney, the course instructor, has as one of her goals that her students understand early childhood development from the point of view of the child — that they see the early childhood classroom not as the teacher's classroom but as the child's. As a means to this end, she's exploring the use of narrative and drama as tools for learning, which has been pioneered by Vivian Paley and now is becoming a significant feature of some early childhood classrooms.

Our work with Peggy is part of an action research project — one of several that Peggy has undertaken over the past few years in her ongoing effort to transform her own pedagogy. She's actually teaching two sections of the course, so there's a comparative aspect to the project.

The collaborative team

In order to look more closely at whether students are meeting her goals for them, Peggy has invited two of us to observe and work with her. My involvement is a function of the fact that she wanted to incorporate some further writing in the class. The other colleague, Karen Williams, is an early childhood specialist from the home ec department.

Our task is to work with Peggy to see whether we can find evidence that her students are coming to understand what it means to see the early childhood classroom from the child's point of view, *and* to look at what she's doing, instructionally, that helps or hampers that end. Along the way, we provide feedback Peggy can use to make mid-course adjustments and improvements.

The design of our study

The design begins with what students in the course are doing, which is to choose one child in an early childhood classroom to observe for eight weeks. Every week students take extensive field notes on "their child," and then in class they choose a small piece of what happened during the hour-long observation and craft it into a story, which another student — their partner — "scripts" into a drama. Then the story/drama is acted out. The student's partner serves as narrator, reading the script, while others serve as impromptu actors. Importantly, the student whose observation the drama is based on acts out the role of the child.

This process occurs on a regular, biweekly basis. The dramas take up the first hour of class; in the second, students work to pull out of those dramas common threads and themes related to early childhood development.

In addition, in every class session, Peggy asks students to write a short formative evaluation of some aspect of the course — how they think the dramas are working, or how well discussion is going. . . . These evaluations provide further grist for our research together.

Our roles

Our inquiry process more or less parallels what students in the course are doing. They observe children in an early childhood classroom and take detailed field notes; we observe and take field notes about Peggy's class. Karen and I alternate doing this, each of us observing four times, every other week, for a total of eight weeks. Every two weeks, we get together to discuss our field notes. We haven't actually turned our notes into dramas, as Peggy's students have, but we sometimes find ourselves telling stories about what we've observed.

The three of us also read the formative evaluations students write in each class, and Peggy is keeping a journal every day after class. So we have a lot of material to draw from. Eventually our work together will probably lead to a collaborative article.

What we're learning

My job is to help faculty develop writing assignments for all kinds of courses, so one of my interests is in seeing how the three kinds of writing work — the field notes, dramas, and formative evaluations. I'm interested in seeing how students' writing changes during the semester, and in my role as director of the Writing Center I'm interested in how other faculty might take advantage of these strategies. But I'm also thinking about using them myself in my own teaching. In a course on literacy that I will be teaching next year, my students will be writing literacy narratives and observing the literacy practices of others. I will incorporate the scripting and acting of dramatic narratives into my class so that we can more immediately know the varieties of literacy narratives.

Karen is teaching a class that's a companion to Peggy's, and they have a number of students in common. As you'd expect, the collaboration has prompted lots of discussion of those students. But it also gets us talking about issues of curricular clustering and sequencing — about the connections between and among courses. Certainly our conversations have strengthened the links between Peggy's and Karen's courses.

For Peggy, I think, the main benefit of the collaboration is that she has constant feedback, from students and from Karen and me, which allows her to make ongoing adjustments and corrections in what she's doing — very nuanced things having to do with the internal rhythms of the class period, for instance. She'll also be able to use what we're learning to shape subsequent semesters.

For all three of us there's also a kind of side benefit, which is that we always end up talking about our *own* teaching.

Issues

One issue is ethical: Peggy has asked her students if Karen and I can come to the class and observe. This is qualitative research ethics.

Secondly, there's an interesting issue about whether the observer should get involved or intervene in the activity being observed. In fact, this was an issue both for Peggy's students and for Karen and me. We didn't settle the issue, but we did find that on occasion it seemed possible — even necessary — to play both roles at once, observer and participant.

Finally there's an issue about transferability: Is the observation and enactment process that Peggy has her students using one that could be used more generally, in other classes and fields of study? It seems to me the answer is yes, especially in courses that entail some kind of observation of human behavior — say in sociology or psychology. I'm particularly excited, myself, about having students learn how to take detailed field notes, a process that was new to me and very powerful, especially when done over time, as our observations of Peggy were.

Perhaps the most powerful feature of this project has been the nature of collaboration. We are not team teaching or even teaching collaboratively. Instead, we are *studying* teaching collaboratively, with both immediate and long-range effects on all of our teaching.

Facing questions about his own teaching that might well have significance for others in the department, John Wright, a participant in AAHE's project on the peer review of teaching at the University of Wisconsin-Madison, teamed up with a colleague to do a comparative study of two sections of a chemistry course, employing two different pedagogical approaches. Funding for the effort was provided through the National Science Foundation, the Advanced Research Projects Agency, and the University of Wisconsin-Madison Chancellor's Office. John describes the study's purposes, methods, and findings to date.

A COLLABORATIVE, COMPARATIVE STUDY OF STUDENT LEARNING IN CHEMISTRY AT THE UNIVERSITY OF WISCONSIN-MADISON

by John Wright, Faculty Member, Department of Chemistry,
University of Wisconsin-Madison

This collaborative project started because I had questions about whether the things that I was doing in my course in analytical and equilibrium chemistry were worth it. The questions were important for me personally because I wanted to find out whether it was worth my time undertaking various innovations in my teaching. If the innovations weren't really contributing something significant to the students' skill level, then I didn't want to be bothered.

In addition, I knew that many of my colleagues had the same questions about their *own* teaching, so I wanted to undertake this study in a way that would be both credible and reliable in their eyes. The way to do so, I thought, was to work collaboratively with another faculty member whose section would be the comparison group.

What we wanted to find out

Sometime ago, I became unhappy with the performance of students as they came out of my course. I thought I was teaching a good course, but at the end of the semester I could see that students didn't have the grasp of the material that you would have hoped. Even *A* students. They could apply course material in the contexts I gave it to them, but if we talked about the same material in a different context, they really floundered. It was my hypothesis that the reason for this failure was that students hadn't really struggled with the course material in their own terms.

So I set about changing my course so that students had the opportunity to struggle with it on their own. It's hard to describe the character of the change, actually, because it was really lots of interrelated changes. I started using student groups. And I incorporated computers to help students apply simple concepts in more difficult, authentic kinds of chemical problems. Students would read research papers together and answer questions that ranged from showing that they understood what the paper said to coming up with innovative ways of applying what was in the paper to some other practical problem. Then we worked on open-ended projects where I would give them a goal and it was up to them to design some approach that would meet that goal, and then they would have to implement it, make it work, write it up, analyze it, and defend it. We had cooperative examinations that were a lot harder than I would have given such students before. We had an absolute grading scale, but we also had students evaluate one another: They could give bonus points if there was somebody in the class who was especially helpful to them.

So there was a lot of work going on in the class that put the focus on group learning and solving tough problems.

More generally, I took the focus off myself as the teacher and tried to put more of the burden of learning on the student. And this of course changed the atmosphere of the classroom in fundamental ways. I tried to give them more responsibility, but also the support that they needed to accomplish things, so that they realized that if they were willing to work in the class, they were going to get an *A*.

This new approach seemed to be working. The students were really impressive; I was blown away by the creativity and competence some of them brought to course projects. They had a deep command of the material, and they could apply it in different contexts in very creative ways. In short, student performance was at a level far above what I'd seen before. And they were really enjoying the course, saying it made a real difference in their lives.

But is it working?

But all of this is mostly just personal observation. When I told other faculty members about what I was doing, they would nod their heads and say, "Yes, we understand, and we believe you" . . . and "You're doing great, John, but I don't see how I can do this in my class." They wanted to see evidence that these students were really better than they were before — not just that they *liked* the new approach. There was a sense among some of my colleagues that the course engendered lots of student energy and excitement but no real substance. No meat.

I wanted to be able to address my colleagues' questions and skepticism — and I wanted to be able to answer their questions for myself, as well. So that's what led to this quite ambitious collaborative evaluation project: We needed something that would provide hard, objective facts.

A collaborative study

In thinking about how to answer my own and my colleagues' questions, I thought of a comparative study, in which my section of the course would be compared with a section taught by a colleague — R. Claude Woods — who is a superb scholar-teacher. When chemistry students graduate, they often remark on how skillful Claude is. As someone who cares deeply about teaching, Claude would, I thought, be intrigued by this teaching experiment, and I knew that he had the self-confidence to join in.

What was also significant about our partnership was that I knew that with his as a "control section," I was setting a high standard against which to compare my own methods.

The idea was not to find out who was better but to cooperate in a study that might tell us about the impact of Claude's fairly traditional lecture-based approach and my more student-centered approach.

The design of the study

What we decided to do was a two-pronged study of my course. Staff from UW-Madison's LEAD (Learning Through Evaluation, Adaptation, and Dissemination) Center were vital partners in this effort. The Center is predicated on the idea that you can apply investigative methods from anthropology to educational settings and questions, and its aim was to learn about the culture of the course, and the relationships among individuals in it. Center staff really permeated the two classrooms and the laboratories, watching what went on, and talking to students alone and in groups, both from my section and Claude's. The LEAD Center also conducted open-ended, structured interviews with a substantial sample of the students in both Claude's and my sections.

Then, in addition, we had at the end of the semester an evaluation of my students by a set of twenty-five faculty from outside chemistry; they were charged with assessing the competence of students from the two sections and seeing whether they could distinguish a difference between them that was meaningful. This aspect of the study was designed to give us insights about the impact of the two approaches on students, and also to give other faculty an experience of collaborating in this kind of study.

Conclusions

We haven't fully completed the study. We generated mountains of data, and we're still sorting through them in order to draw final conclusions. We want to make certain that we do this right and that faculty feel that our study of teaching is done with the same rigor we apply to our research.

But already it's possible to point to several areas of impact.

Impact

First, the project has had a benefit for me, confirming my impression that these teaching innovations really are working — that they're worth it.

Second, the faculty who conducted the interviews had a chance to talk with one another about their roles and protocols. They did this in training sessions conducted by a faculty member outside of chemistry. By report, there was a lot of enthusiasm among the faculty who did the interviews; they thought it was a cool experiment, and they were excited about participating in it. It got people excited about peer collaboration and review of teaching.

Finally, for some of us in the department, at least, this project confirmed the importance of systematic, collaborative inquiry into teaching and learning.

RESOURCES

Austin, Ann E., and Roger G. Baldwin. *Faculty Collaboration: Enhancing the Quality of Scholarship and Teaching.* ASHE-ERIC Higher Education Report, no. 7. Washington, DC: The George Washington University School of Education and Human Development, 1991.

Deals more extensively with collaboration in research, but accounts of trends and issues pertain to teaching, as well. One section focuses on collaborative teaching ventures and their outcomes. To advance effective collaboration, a final chapter puts forward recommendations for faculty, administrators, and higher education as a field.

hooks, bell. *Teaching to Transgress: Education as the Practice of Freedom.* New York: Routledge, 1994.

Weimer, Maryellen. "The Disciplinary Journals on Pedagogy." *Change* 25 (6): 44-51 (November/December 1993).

Weimer comments in depth on three of the more well established discipline-based teaching journals (*Journal of Marketing Education, Teaching of Psychology,* and *Journal of College Science Teaching*), but also looks at the character of our published discourse about pedagogy more generally, calling for less imitation of traditional social science and more attention to alternative but rigorous forms and genres for representing what teachers know and do. The article ends with a thoughtful set of recommendations, which speak not only to the editors of these journals but to faculty wishing to direct their scholarship in this direction.

DEPARTMENTAL OCCASIONS FOR COLLABORATION

Many of the strategies featured in earlier chapters of this book can be used by individuals who have the inclination and persistence to find a colleague or two and "just do it." But a different route to change is through strategies that involve the department *qua* department — strategies embedded in or connected to policies and processes that in some way or another involve the collective faculty.

This chapter features three strategies that meet this test: a pedagogical colloquium used in faculty hiring, a professional development program for graduate students, and a departmental course-files collection, or teaching library. And, you'll find a checklist for assessing a department's overall "system" for monitoring and ensuring the quality of teaching and learning.

FACULTY REPORT

In conjunction with its participation in the AAHE project on the peer review of teaching, the history department at Stanford has been piloting an adaptation of what Lee Shulman calls the "pedagogical colloquium." An addition to the usual "job-talk," the pedagogical colloquium is aimed at getting better evidence about teaching into decisions about hiring new faculty. As Richard Roberts's report below makes clear, one benefit of such a process is that it introduces teaching effectiveness as an explicit expectation for new hires. Equally important, it prompts conversation among current faculty about the nature of those expectations and how the department defines good teaching.

THE PEDAGOGICAL COLLOQUIUM: FOCUSING ON TEACHING IN THE HIRING PROCESS IN THE STANFORD UNIVERSITY HISTORY DEPARTMENT

by Richard Roberts, Faculty Member, Department of History, Stanford University

One of the results of participation in AAHE's peer review of teaching project was that I put forward to the history department a set of suggestions for raising the level of attention to teaching. One suggestion focused on the fact that the department was about to embark on three or four searches, and we saw an opportunity to get our candidates to talk about teaching in a way that hadn't been possible in our previous context of the "job talk" as a formal lecture on the candidate's research interest. The research presentation had served us well in giving a sense of the candidate's intellectual reach, but it was not at all clear that it was a sufficient test of the capacity to teach in a variety of settings.

Our purpose

What we did, then, was to propose that all our candidates engage not only in the traditional job talk but in an "informal discussion about teaching and curriculum" — a phrase we chose because the more formal "pedagogical colloquium" label raised concerns among my colleagues that they themselves did not have a clearly defined theory of teaching or pedagogy, and that there was no way we could ask freshly minted PhDs to lay out their philosophy of teaching in formal, theoretical terms.

Our aim was to assess in our "informal discussion" the degree to which candidates were actively engaged with teaching and how they thought about making available to students the kinds of intellectual interests in the field that they themselves were pursuing as scholars.

How we ran our "informal discussion about teaching and curriculum"

Candidates were told in advance that this new pedagogical discussion would take place; they were encouraged to prepare for it by putting together syllabi for courses they might teach and to take a look at the curriculum we offer. What we wanted to do was to see how candidates would fit into the teaching enterprise that we already have, and how they would build on and contribute to it.

The discussion lasted an hour and a half. We began by asking about courses the candidate would want to teach, and ranged, from there, to questions about teaching graduates and undergraduates, and about how the courses he or she might propose would fit into the Stanford curriculum.

We were especially interested in the candidate's comments on how he or she would teach a particular book — or sequence of books, or methodological debate — which was *very* revealing.

Impact on the hiring process

First, let me say that the candidates themselves — even one who had very little teaching experience — thought the pedagogical discussion was a terrific idea.

My colleagues, too, were largely persuaded. While at the outset they rather grudgingly accepted this addition to the usual job talk, it was clear that the new occasion provided important information that the department considered in making appointments. For instance, there was one candidate who gave a good — a very good — job talk; the research was really very well honed. But when it came to talking about teaching, it became clear that this candidate had put very little time into thinking about teaching. The search committee took this information into consideration when advancing a finalist to the department.

In another case, the teaching discussion kept a candidate in the running when the job talk was less than stupendous.

Impact on the culture of the department

First, the new discussion of teaching and curriculum was an occasion for important conversation among department members — especially as we evaluated candidates — that had not regularly occurred in the past. One of the most important aspects of the experience was the excitement on the part of faculty attending the discussion.

Second, the experience was good for our graduate students, who were encouraged to attend. They saw our candidates as potential teachers whose abilities they could evaluate, and, perhaps more important, they saw that talking about teaching and being thoughtful about it was one of the kinds of things that is likely to be expected of *them* when they go on the job market.

"IF WE REALLY WANT A DIFFERENT KIND OF CULTURE, WE OUGHT TO CHANGE OUR ADVERTISING. BY WAY OF EXAMPLE, I'VE DRAFTED AN AD FOR *THE CHRONICLE* ANNOUNCING A NEW POSITION IN 20TH CENTURY U.S. HISTORY AT SHULMAN COLLEGE. 'WE SEEK A NEW FACULTY MEMBER WHO IS GOOD AT BOTH RESEARCH AND TEACHING' — THE AD SAYS THE USUAL THINGS ALONG THOSE LINES. BUT THEN IT GOES ON TO SAY THAT CANDIDATES WHO ARE INVITED TO CAMPUS WILL BE ASKED TO OFFER TWO COLLOQUIA. IN ONE COLLOQUIUM, THEY WILL DESCRIBE THEIR CURRENT RESEARCH — THE USUAL RESEARCH COLLOQUIUM. IN THE SECOND, WHICH WE'LL CALL THE *PEDAGOGICAL COLLOQUIUM,* THEY WILL ADDRESS THE PEDAGOGY OF THEIR DISCIPLINE. THEY WILL DO SO BY EXPOUNDING ON THE DESIGN OF A COURSE, SHOWING SYSTEMATICALLY HOW THIS COURSE . . . REPRESENTS THE CENTRAL ISSUES IN THE DISCIPLINE AND HOW IN ITS PEDAGOGY IT AFFORDS STUDENTS THE OPPORTUNITY TO ENGAGE IN THE INTELLECTUAL AND MORAL WORK OF THE DISCIPLINE."

— Lee Shulman (1993), p. 7

With this in mind, I'm introducing a series of workshops for graduate students to help them prepare for the job market — helping them put together materials about their teaching that will be useful in searches.

Issues to consider

One issue we were very concerned about was that our "informal discussion" not discriminate against candidates who had — through no fault of their own — little teaching experience. We didn't want to favor only those who had several years of teaching experience and could talk more eloquently about it. This turned out not to be a problem in the case of one candidate who had done almost no teaching but who had prepared wonderfully for the discussion and did a superb job of talking about the kinds of teaching that she would like to do. Nevertheless, this is probably an issue to keep in mind in the future, and to stay vigilant about.

Next steps

We have another series of searches coming up, and my expectation is that we will continue to employ the "informal discussion about teaching and curriculum" as part of the search process. It was instituted as a departmental experiment, so we'll revisit the topic, but my sense is that we'll stay with it.

The real question for the future, though, is how sustained the change will be — what linkages the search process will have with the culture of the department. Frankly, I'm doubtful that it will have any sustained impact without systematic follow-through, which means attention to teaching not just at the moment of hire but beyond that, through the ways it is evaluated for instance . . . and that will require stronger signals from upper-level administration. Without such signals, teaching will continue to be seen by many faculty in the department as a private, individual activity, not as a central aspect of the wider university culture.

FACULTY REPORT

With concerns in the air about the quality of undergraduate education on the one hand, and the preparation of the future professoriate on the other, departments on many campuses are ratcheting up their attention to the teaching experiences of graduate students. As reported below by Geoffrey Chase, a series of activities for graduate assistants in the writing program at Northern Arizona University helps them develop teaching skills but also inculcates habits of collaboration and exchange that are beginning to affect the larger culture of the department, as well.

A PROFESSIONAL DEVELOPMENT PROGRAM FOR GRADUATE STUDENTS: FOSTERING COLLABORATION IN THE WRITING PROGRAM AT NORTHERN ARIZONA UNIVERSITY

by Geoffrey Chase, Director of English Composition, Northern Arizona University

I remember at the end of this past semester, when GAs in our program trickled into the composition office to turn in final grades. One of them, Toni Lefton, a poet, stopped to tell me how impressed she was with the writing that Joy's students had done that term. According to Toni, Joy Janzen, a Ph.D. candidate in applied linguistics, had done a particularly good job of helping students improve their analytical writing in response to the assigned readings in the course. At the same time, Joy, I learned, was impressed with the descriptive writing that Toni's students had done. Toni went on to say that she and Joy had agreed to sit in on each other's classes in the upcoming term, because they recognized they could each learn something about teaching writing from the other.

Teaching as a public act

I had not heard Lee Shulman's term about teaching as "community property," but the idea is very close to the motto that underlies our graduate assistant training program: "Teaching is a public act." When we award a teaching assistantship, whether the recipient has prior teaching experience or not, we believe that he or she will bring distinct qualities and strengths to our program. Further, we're convinced that perhaps the most effective way for teachers to develop is for them to share what they do best at the same time they draw on others' strengths.

With this view in mind, we have developed a range of strategies for ensuring that the public nature of what we do in the composition classroom is central to our program. Our goal is to provide as many opportunities for exchange and collaboration as possible.

The syllabus as a common frame of reference

We begin by asking that all of our graduate assistants teach from standard syllabi. Thematically focused on the environment or on academic culture, our shared syllabi provide the basis for graduate assistants to exchange concrete ideas, suggestions, and lesson plans that are consistent with the overall objective of the course, as well as immediately useful for, say, teaching a chapter of Rachel Carson's *Silent Spring,* or to help students understand the demands of analyzing an essay by Annie Dillard. Because all students face the same tasks and assignments, such information is immediately and widely helpful.

Our graduate students come from a range of academic backgrounds — some in applied linguistics, others in poetry, and everything in between — and they bring their own training to bear on the demands of teaching a required composition course. The common syllabi they share while teaching in our program thus become an important point of connection and a vital part of their shared experience.

Mentoring and collegiality

In addition to standard syllabi, we have implemented a mentoring system that encourages collaboration and exchange. During their first semester in our program, all new graduate teaching assistants work closely with an experienced graduate assistant who serves as a mentor. Mentors sit in on the new GA's classes at least once a week, the new graduate assistant has the opportunity to sit in on the mentor's classes, and the two meet in weekly small groups with others to discuss the joys and difficulties of teaching a required composition course.

We strive to keep this mentoring on a collaborative, collegial level. Mentors, for example, are never asked to evaluate new GAs, and the meetings they hold with new GAs frequently take place at local restaurants or coffee shops. The mentoring program complements in a practical way the training that occurs before the start of the semester and that continues in a weekly practicum in which new GAs develop and present lesson plans for upcoming weeks. It also provides an anchor for the new graduate assistants, giving them a strong connection to the program and to one another.

Collaborating in the assessment of student work

We have also developed a portfolio system that allows GAs to evaluate student work together. At mid-term and at the end of every semester, GAs devote a day to norming and evaluation of student work. As GAs norm "anchor portfolios" and then move on to evaluate what students across the program have submitted, they grapple together with how to apply the agreed-upon evaluation criteria and how to provide students with useful feedback. They argue about difficult portfolios (the one in which a Native American student writes beautiful descriptive essays but still struggles with analytical writing, or ones by students who have rewritten and revised many times but still fall below the level of acceptable college writing). They also discuss the outstanding portfolios, and talk about what kinds of feedback will be best for really excellent writers.

Evaluation and assessment thus become topics of conversation, publicly debated — not tasks reserved for a private interaction between a single student and a single instructor. One consequence is that evaluation in our program has a fairly high consistency across sections. Another is that GAs have an opportunity to develop more clearly their own sense of how to evaluate and respond to student work by drawing on the suggestions and ideas of others.

> **Characteristics of Departments That Support Teaching Excellence**
> Based on interviews with 300 faculty in twenty diverse colleges and universities, research from the Stanford Institute for Higher Education Research has uncovered common characteristics of departments that place collective emphasis on teaching excellence:
>
> "The exemplary departments are distinguished by their supportive culture for undergraduate teaching, frequent interaction among faculty, tolerance of differences, generational equity, workload equity, and course rotation. Also important are peer as well as serious student teaching evaluation, balanced incentives, consensus decision-making, and, above all, effective department chairs" (Massy, Wilger, and Colbeck, 1994, p. 14).

Teaching portfolios

Finally, we have all the graduate assistants prepare teaching portfolios, which are shared with others at the end of their first semester of teaching. The portfolio is assigned early in their program to help them become more reflective about their teaching and the intellectual nature of what they do in the classroom. Then, in subsequent semesters of teaching, they update, revise, and further develop their portfolios.

Throughout the portfolio-development process, the purpose is growth and development; we do not use them for evaluation. We also show teaching portfolios by experienced GAs as a means of raising questions with those just beginning about how they can develop more fully the vital interplay between teaching and scholarship.

Of course, once a graduate student leaves our program, this "teaching development" portfolio takes on another function, and may help our graduates secure jobs.

Collaboration on three levels

The upshot of all this is that our GAs share their work as teachers on three levels: planning, implementation, and assessment. They read one another's lesson plans, they sit in on one another's classes, and they read and discuss together the work their students have done. As a result they are stronger teachers. In fact, last year when our graduate college gave awards to the best graduate assistants on campus, ten of sixteen awards went to GAs in the English department.

Impact on the department

The training program for graduate assistants has been in effect for a relatively brief time — two and a half years. Thus, we are still in the process of determining its effect on the English department as a whole. Even in this brief time, however, several faculty have noted a rise in the level of professionalism exhibited by graduate assistants, and some have worked with graduate students to develop collaborative research projects related to composition pedagogy. Thus, the level of sharing and collaboration that occurs within our training program has started to ripple out to include faculty.

So far, only a few faculty have actually taught in our composition program. Those who have, however, have taken part in the training sessions we offer, met with graduate students and their mentors, and clearly become an integral part of the program. At the conclusion of their teaching experience, these faculty have gone on to praise the level of collaboration that exists through the program, and they have talked about how much their teaching, both in and outside of the composition program, has been informed and improved by that experience.

FACULTY REPORT

A number of participant departments in AAHE's peer review of teaching project proposed the seemingly simple but powerful idea of establishing a departmental teaching library, or (as it's called in the example that follows) "course file." The idea here is local materials — that is, not a book shelf with the ten best books on teaching (also a good idea) but a collection of the faculty's own syllabi, exams, student projects, and the like, available for public examination, borrowing, and adaptation. Charles Burnap, of UNC at Charlotte, explains how he and his mathematics department colleagues have begun developing such a collection.

THE DEPARTMENTAL TEACHING LIBRARY: A MATHEMATICS COURSE FILE AT THE UNIVERSITY OF NORTH CAROLINA AT CHARLOTTE

by Charles Burnap, Faculty Member, Department of Mathematics, University of North Carolina at Charlotte

In our AAHE peer review of teaching project proposal we included a recommendation to departmental colleagues encouraging the exchange of information about all mathematics courses, particularly those at the upper division. To this end, we have established a file of course portfolios in the mathematics department main office.

To compile the files, we asked teachers to complete the following information for each of their courses:

1) What book did you use?

2) What syllabus did you follow? Did you omit any sections? If so, which?

3) Did you have specific goals in mind when you taught this course? Overall, was the course successful?

4) What were the strong and weak points of the chosen text? Would you use this book again? If not, can you suggest an alternative?

5) Comment on the syllabus. Which material or sections form the core of the course? Should the syllabus be changed?

6) Did you use technological aids (e.g., calculators or symbolic manipulators)? If so, which ones? Did their use enhance the course?

7) Did you hand out any supplemental material that was particularly helpful?

8) Did you approach certain material or sections in a particularly successful way? (Please illustrate so that others may benefit from your experience.)

9) Including sample tests and/or quizzes would also be helpful.

Arranged by course, rather than by instructor, the files reinforce our emphasis on collective rather than individual responsibility for the quality of teaching and learning. All our mathematics teachers have access to the files.

ASSESSING THE DEPARTMENT'S SYSTEM FOR ENSURING AND IMPROVING THE QUALITY OF TEACHING AND LEARNING

Robert Zemsky (Pew, 1996) argues that the department or academic program (which might in fact be interdisciplinary) is a key unit for the kind of "restructuring" that's so much in the academic air today. At least on larger campuses, the department or program is where a sense of collective responsibility is — or is not — enacted, and where the possibility of collegiality around teaching and learning as scholarly activity must be cultivated.

This, in fact, is a central premise of AAHE's project on the peer review of teaching, which is organized around pilot departments. A fundamental premise of the project — confirmed now by several years of experience — is that strategies for peer collaboration and review must be shaped by the discipline and adapted to the departmental culture; that what works in English or sociology may be quite different from what makes sense in chemistry or business. And this is very much what we've seen: One participating history department, for instance, has argued for the course portfolio as a cousin to the case-study approach employed by historians, the portfolio being a kind of history of a course. One business department plan includes the use of faculty "focus groups" to ascertain what issues about teaching and its peer review the department would most like to address.

This is not to suggest that the department is the only relevant unit for engaging colleagues in various strategies for peer collaboration and review of teaching; good things happen among colleagues from different disciplines, as well. But on most campuses the department is a good place to focus, and the accompanying checklist (see box) — developed through the AAHE project — can serve as a useful conversation starter for a departmental meeting or retreat. It's designed, as you'll see, not only to describe current conditions but to suggest new possibilities.

RESOURCES

Byrnes, Heidi. "Faculty Hiring: One Department's Experience." *AAHE Bulletin* 47 (9): 7, 9-10 (May 1995).

> A companion to Shulman's, listed below, Byrnes's piece describes in some detail how the Department of German at Georgetown University adapted the concept of the pedagogical colloquium — creating not a separate occasion focused on teaching but an integrated experience in which the candidate talks first about his or her intellectual history (ten minutes), then briefly about recent scholarly work, then about teaching; audience members then engage the candidate in discussion. Byrnes reports positive effects on hiring decisions and on departmental culture, echoing many of the points Richard Roberts makes in this chapter.

From Idea to Prototype: The Peer Review of Teaching: A Project Workbook, edited by Pat Hutchings. Washington, DC: American Association for Higher Education, 1995.

> The checklist on p. 90 was adapted from "Guidelines for Department Projects," located behind Tab 5.

Kennedy, Donald. "Another Century's End, Another Revolution for Higher Education." *Change* 27 (3): 8-15 (May/June 1995).

> Kennedy's piece puts a larger context around strategies reported on in this chapter, looking at the considerable leverage for change in the reform of graduate education. In this spirit, he calls for greater attention to the preparation of graduate students for their multiple faculty roles — and especially teaching, and describes the graduate student seminar he himself teaches at Stanford University to prepare graduate students for professorial life.

Making Teaching Community Property: The Faculty Role in Ensuring and Improving the Quality of Teaching and Learning

Which of the following statements describe the department's existing policies, practices, and culture?

❏ There are clear expectations about what constitutes effective teaching; i.e., faculty understand what the department values when it comes to teaching and student learning.

❏ Expectations for teaching effectiveness reflect a sense of development; i.e., criteria for effective teaching at the full professor rank are different from those for assistant professors.

❏ Faculty receive useful feedback about their teaching at appropriate points; assistance is provided in making use of feedback for improvement.

❏ Processes and policies for the review and evaluation of teaching encourage pedagogical experimentation, risk taking, efforts to improve. . . .

❏ There are mechanisms for asking not only about individual teaching effectiveness but about the department's collective impact on student learning.

❏ Good talk about teaching and learning is common; "student bashing" is rare.

❏ There are formal/regular occasions for taking up issues, opportunities, and problems related to the quality of teaching and learning.

❏ Formal procedures for the evaluation of teaching promote rather than discourage meaningful exchange and debate about teaching and learning.

❏ In general, faculty believe that the department's policies and practices related to the quality of teaching are fair.

— adapted from *From Idea to Prototype*

Lambert, Leo M., and Stacey Lane Tice. *Preparing Graduate Students to Teach: A Guide to Programs That Improve Undergraduate Education and Develop Tomorrow's Faculty.* Washington, DC: American Association for Higher Education, 1993.

Contains descriptions of numerous centralized and department-based programs, many of which, like that described by Geoffrey Chase in this chapter, include multiple strategies to foster collaboration and publicness about teaching.

Massy, William F., Andrea K. Wilger, and Carol Colbeck. "Overcoming 'Hollowed' Collegiality." *Change* 26 (4): 10-20 (July/August 1994).

Drawing on interviews with 300 faculty across twenty institutions, the authors identify obstacles to collegiality (including the superficial assessment of teaching) and then describe eleven characteristics of departments that "support effective teaching," which include substantive, fair evaluation of teaching and balanced incentives. The role of chairs is also emphasized. A useful template to hold up against one's own department culture.

Pew Higher Education Roundtable. "Double Agent." *Policy Perspectives* 6 (3): 1-11 (February 1996).

The essay grows out of a special roundtable convened by the Pew Higher Education Roundtable. For several years, AAHE and Pew Roundtable publications have argued that the academic department, as a "producer's cooperative," ought to take broad responsibility for the quality of services it provides. A department should be held accountable for the quality of teaching its members deliver, for the coherence of its major, for its contributions to the general education curriculum, and for the supervision and rewarding of its individual faculty members. This essay extends those concepts by sketching contours of the department as it could become: the principal agent for the purposeful recasting of American higher education.

Shulman, Lee. "Faculty Hiring: The Pedagogical Colloquium: Three Models." *AAHE Bulletin* 47 (9): 6-9 (May 1995).

Having proposed the idea of the pedagogical colloquium in an earlier piece (see "Teaching as Community Property" below), Shulman here suggests three protocols for its conduct. "One of the puzzlements about the pedagogical colloquium," he writes, "is what, exactly, we would want the candidate to talk about." Three possible models are then presented: the course narrative, in which the candidate explains the shape or "argument" of a selected course/syllabus; the colloquium in which the candidate talks about how to teach a key concept or idea in the field; and the dilemma-centered colloquium, in which the candidate reflects publicly on some problematic aspect of teaching — e.g., the right balance between breadth and depth. An excellent resource for departments who want to try out the "pc."

————— . "Teaching as Community Property: Putting an End to Pedagogical Solitude." *Change* 25 (6): 6-7 (November/December 1993).

Wergin, Jon F. *The Collaborative Department: How Five Campuses Are Inching Toward Cultures of Collective Responsibility*. Washington, DC: American Association for Higher Education, 1994.

> The bulk of Wergin's monograph comprises five case studies: Kent State University, Rochester Institute of Technology (College of Business), Syracuse University (The Maxwell School), UC-Berkeley (College of Natural Resources), and University of Wisconsin-Madison (College of Letters and Science). Wergin's analysis of what the five case studies suggest points to several issues related to this volume, including the evaluation of individual work in light of group purposes and goals, and the evaluation and reward of collective productivity in teaching and other faculty activities.

CHAPTER 9

INTERCAMPUS COLLABORATION
AND EXTERNAL REVIEW OF TEACHING

We have all heard the argument that teaching suffers from being a purely local activity, while research is national and international. In fact, many of the issues of teaching and learning that most need attention *are* local issues, since it's not teaching in general but teaching in particular — *this* course to *these* students — where the rubber meets the road. Nevertheless, some aspects of teaching would benefit from a larger, more-than-local community of interest. These include aspects of course design, the development of curricular materials, and, increasingly, instructional uses of technology.

This chapter focuses on strategies for collaboration with peers beyond the institution, looking first at discipline-based conversation groups many faculty are tapping into through the Internet, then at steps toward the external peer review of teaching, as reported by several faculty.

BUILDING LARGER COMMUNITIES OF INTEREST: DISCIPLINE-BASED, ONLINE CONVERSATIONS ABOUT TEACHING AND LEARNING

Faculty looking for good colleagues on issues of teaching and learning may, increasingly these days, find them not in the next office but across the country — or even across the world — through online, discipline-based conversations.

Historians for example, find one another through H-Teach, a listserv operated out of Michigan State University focused on teaching college history. H-Teach is one of seventy-three electronic discussion groups for scholars in the humanities and social sciences supported by the National Endowment for the Humanities, "to provide a positive, supportive, equalitarian environment for the friendly exchange of ideas and scholarly resources."

In chemistry, colleagues gather on ChemEd, an electronic discussion group run out of the University of West Florida for chemists who want to dis-

Some Online Conversations

In history . . .
To subscribe to H-Teach, a listserv for faculty interested in the teaching and learning of history at the college level, send the message:
> subscribe H-Teach yourfirstname yourlastname

to the address:
> listserv@msu.edu

If your interest is in the U.S. history survey course, you may wish to join H-Survey. To subscribe, send the message:
> subscribe H-Survey yourfirstname yourlastname

to the address:
> listserv@msu.edu

In chemistry . . .
For discussion of current problems, ideas, and questions in chemistry education, you may wish to subscribe to the ChemEd listserv. To do so, send the message:
> SUBSCRIBE CHEMED-L YOURFIRSTNAME YOURLASTNAME

to the address:
> LISTSERV@UWF.CC.UWF.EDU or LISTSERV@UWF.BITNET

In computer science . . .
The Computer Science Discipline Network operates both a listserv and a WWW site. To subscribe to the listserv, send the message:
> subscribe csdn-teaching

to the address:
> list-manager@ukc.ac.uk

The WWW address is:
> http://www.ukc.ac.uk/CSDN/

cuss teaching and learning issues. Topics are far ranging, from options for teaching difficult concepts in introductory chemistry, to placement testing, to uses of instructional technology in chemistry. Katharine Covert, assistant professor of chemistry at West Virginia University, reports, "One of the best things about the ChemEd list is that the participants are very diverse — from community colleges and high schools as well as high-powered universities. And it does my pretenure heart good when I recognize a 'name' from the research journals who is also subscribed to ChemEd. It makes me think that maybe I can do both, as well."

Great Britain's Computer Science Discipline Network offers a listserv, plus other strategies for collaboration. The Network is administered from the University of Kent, by Sally Fincher, who reports that it is one of twenty-four Discipline Networks recently set up under an initiative by the government's Department of Education and Employment. CSDN has (1) an electronic listserv on which a new topic or issue relevant to teaching and learning is raised every month, (2) a World Wide Web site on which previous discussions from the mailing list are archived, and new resources and materials are made available, and (3) periodic face-to-face events.

These three examples are, as you would imagine, the merest tip of the iceberg. In response to a request for such examples posted last fall on AAHE's listserv on instructional uses of technology, I got literally dozens of responses from faculty across the country, in a wide range of disciplines, who are using technology to advance discussion of pedagogical issues, to work with colleagues elsewhere on courseware development, and to promote professional development. Their conversations constitute significant communities of discourse about teaching, and are in this sense a sort of foundation for the eventual external peer review of teaching that is featured in the following two Faculty Reports.

Fostering Communities of Discourse About Teaching

"The existence of an accepted procedure for assessing productivity and growth in research is made possible, in part, by the fact that each subgroup of researchers — topologists, for instance — forms a naturally connected community. Members of these communities speak the same language and have a common set of standards for judging professional achievement and excellence. In these settings, peer review reflects the natural community of interest.

"One example of a growing 'natural community' in mathematics education is that of faculty involved in the calculus reform movement. The community developed as an outgrowth of a conference, 'Toward a Lean and Lively Calculus,' held at Tulane University in 1986. Members of the community are in agreement that both curriculum and teaching methods for calculus need to be changed, although they are not in total agreement about what those changes should be. They have developed a common language related to calculus reform and attend meetings where they exchange ideas and materials.

"Efforts to document growth in teaching, likewise, can be performed most readily within other similar natural communities. These communities may consist of faculty in similar types of institutions, in institutions that serve similar populations, or in institutions that have some other identifiable linkage. *Fostering natural communities of interest around educational issues can provide a context for peer review and a source for developing a common language for discussion and debate.* Professional organizations and faculty networks such as [Mathematicians for Educational Reform] can contribute to this effort by nurturing natural communities of interest."

— Mathematical Sciences Education Board, p. 15

A component of work to make teaching "community property" in the chemistry department at Indiana University Purdue University Indianapolis has been a pilot effort at external review. As explained below by department chair David Malik, the focus of review has been on the course and course design, rather than all aspects of teaching — a dimension of pedagogy that's particularly appropriate for external review. As David reports, both individuals and the department have benefitted from the effort, which is now expanding to include larger numbers of faculty.

EXTERNAL PEER REVIEW OF TEACHING: A NEW EFFORT IN THE CHEMISTRY DEPARTMENT AT IUPUI

by David Malik, Chair, Department of Chemistry, Indiana University Purdue University Indianapolis

It's important to begin by saying that we're using external review on a pilot basis, for starters among senior faculty — full professors, who have nothing to lose, but who can help us understand how to do this, eventually, perhaps, among a wider group of faculty. In fact, this semester I'm already starting to broaden it out and am looking for volunteers of all ranks, ages, and levels.

The question of documentation

As chair, I have asked faculty to put together documentation that includes the syllabus and a reflective memo about it; ancillary course materials; selected lecture notes; comments on their course goals; and a few other things.

Identifying appropriate external reviewers

This is a new thing, so there's no ready pool out there of people who understand the process and know what to do.

At present, most of our external reviewers are identified by the candidates themselves. Then, in consultation with me or others, the prospects are narrowed down to an appropriate number. I call and ask whether they're willing to do the review, and give them an overview of the project.

What we ask is that outside faculty who are truly peers — people in the same field — react to issues of course content and design as reflected in the materials. The process may not be as "blind" as you'd typically expect in P&T cases, but it's the best arrangement we can manage at this point.

Results and lessons

Our initial foray into external review has turned out to be quite interesting. One faculty member in the department — an analytic chemist — receives a lot of local criticism for the way he conducts one of his courses — what he chooses to include as content. But external review has given us a different perspective. His external reviewers say that his construction of the course represents a new opportunity to teach things that are different from the standard curriculum. One said: This is a good idea, I should do this. One asked: Can I get these materials to use in my own course?

So it's interesting to see that reviewers are gaining something from the process, too. That's a nice fallout from the primary purpose of getting outside comments on the teaching here in our own department.

For faculty participants here at IUPUI, what is probably most valuable — and I would not have anticipated this — is preparing the documentation. That is, the primary benefit is not the feedback from the external reviewer but the process of reflection and self-examination that's required in order to prepare the materials for review. For instance, everyone who has done the reflection on the syllabus has said it was of remarkable benefit in thinking about their course; that they end up verbalizing things that they may not have verbalized or even fully understood before. Faculty are happy about the materials they put together, and the biggest change is to get them thinking more deeply about teaching and sharing their thoughts with others.

People talk about "starting the conversation," and I think that's an outcome of our external review effort.

Fostering leadership in the department

A related kind of benefit that I anticipate pertains to a new mentoring program for junior faculty, focused on teaching. My sense is that folks — mostly senior faculty — who have gone through the reflective process required for external review will be much better mentors — more articulate about what they do, more aware. I think too often we think about teaching as something you *do,* and we don't really reflect on it. It's all doing, no thinking. We're trying to change that.

Problems and issues

External review of teaching is far from widespread practice. When we send documentation to reviewers — even though I spend a fair amount of time explaining to each of them what we're doing and why — they have lots of questions. Sometimes their reviews come back and, though they offer useful endorsements, the analysis is not so thorough as one would hope. This is not all figured out, but we hope our effort will help advance good practice.

A National Network for External Peer Review of Teaching in Sociology
A missing link in more extensive collaboration and review of teaching beyond the local campus setting is a ready pool of appropriate peers. To meet this need, the American Sociological Association is now working to develop a national network of faculty with the appropriate expertise to serve as external reviewers of teaching. "People who are expert in teaching tend to be invisible," says ASA deputy executive director Carla Howery. "So we are trying to locate such people, and to do so in a way that goes beyond self-identification; some corroboration of their expertise will be needed. Eventually, sociology faculty who have made a particular kind of contribution in teaching — for example, designed a simulation — could call ASA and get a list of two to three peers, probably from institutions similar to their own, who might review that work."

For more information, contact: American Sociological Association, 1722 N Street NW, Washington, DC 20036.

Next steps

1) We hope to begin involving junior faculty in the process, giving them this opportunity to generate external evidence of teaching effectiveness.

2) I would like, with faculty permission, eventually to gather all the peer review dossiers (or whatever you want to call them) together in a binder, in a public place, so others can see how the process works, what the materials look like . . . especially junior faculty who may want to sign on to participate.

Chapter 4 of this book describes a process of student interviewing undertaken by Peter Shedd and Jere Morehead in the legal studies program at the University of Georgia. When Jere recently spent a semester at the University of Michigan, the two seized the opportunity to try "long-distance" interviews as a possible component of a protocol for the external peer review of teaching. Jere describes the process and its possibilities.

PILOTING LONG DISTANCE INTERVIEWS WITH STUDENTS AS A POTENTIAL COMPONENT OF THE EXTERNAL PEER REVIEW OF TEACHING

by Jere Morehead, Faculty Member, Department of Insurance, Legal Studies, Real Estate, and Management Science, University of Georgia

On October 31st, 1995, using the videoconferencing technology here at Michigan where I am a visiting professor this semester, I met with five of Peter's students in a business law class at the University of Georgia (a course for senior accounting majors). The technology isn't perfect: There's a two-second delay, which takes a bit of getting used to, but once you get used to that, it's just like you're sitting at a conference table together.

The interview lasted for about an hour, during which I went through a series of questions that Peter and I had agreed on in advance. The students were very interested in talking about testing, since they had recently had an exam in Peter's class, so we had a longer conversation than I had intended on that subject. We covered the other topics, as well.

Two weeks later, using the same technology, Peter met, from Georgia, with six of my students here at Michigan (seniors in a course on the legal environment of business). Again, he used a list of questions that we had agreed upon — questions I was interested in getting answered by students about how the course was progressing.

I should add that both my students and Peter's selected the representatives who would be interviewed.

So that's what we did. It cost about $100 each way, but I understand that the cost is going down.

Our purpose

Peter and I made a presentation on our interviewing of students during a recent national meeting on the peer review of teaching. Our emphasis was on the usefulness of interviews for getting information for improvement. But lots of us at that meeting were also saying that a next step is to create for teaching the kind of peer review that exists in research, which means a process that includes an external dimension. Peter and I thought that long-distance interviews of each other's students would be a step in that direction. We know we can look at each other's dossiers, and we know we can watch a videotape, and so if we added this component of actually talking to students from a distance, we would have the three pieces that we, at least, thought would be necessary to do an external review of teaching similar to what we now do with research.

Of course, Peter and I know each other's teaching pretty well, so the process as we have done it isn't "external" in the usual sense of the word, but we think it could work with faculty who didn't know each other, too. Having someone's dossier of teaching materials and a videotape of his or her class, you could get a sufficient sense of context and background to conduct a useful long-distance interview with a group of students. And if there's a worry about the process being "rigged," there are safeguards as in the review of research, where the department chair or P&T committee puts together the questions and oversees the selection of students who will be interviewed.

I suspect that many institutions now have the technology to make this possible.

Other benefits

Peter and I did these interviews to pilot a process of summative review, but we also learned some things to improve our teaching.

Peter became more aware of a problem that his students had with his tests. The students had some concerns, which I explained to him. Of course, he had his side to the story, but by understanding his students' viewpoint he was able to go back and explain his reasoning to the class and also maybe to modify what he does on the next test a little bit.

As for me, I had a wonderful thing happen. Peter called me the evening after the interview and told me that the only real suggestion students had was that they would love to have me do more small-group work during the class — I hadn't actually done any of this — because they thought it would make everyone more confident in the discussions. Some students felt intimidated about speaking up because they weren't sure their positions were valid. They wanted the opportunity to try out their ideas in small groups of two or three before having to venture an opinion in the larger group and in front of me.

Well, as luck would have it, I had an issue for discussion the next day that was perfect for small groups, so I walked into class the next morning and started with a small-group discussion, which really worked beautifully. The students Peter had interviewed were all sort of smiling during class, and they came up after class and were very appreciative. And, in turn, I could thank *them* for coming up with a good suggestion that I can now make a regular part of class.

Listening to student voices

Now, I know there are people out there who think that students don't know enough to make legitimate suggestions about teaching, and that what I've done is inappropriate catering to them. My response is that it *would* indeed be catering if I did something I didn't actually think was a good idea. But it seemed to me understandable that some students felt intimidated — I call on people at random all during the class. So I saw the suggestion of small groups as a strategy to help them be more involved, to speak up, which they need to do because participation is part of their grade. I took the students' suggestion because it was a good one, not because it would make them happy.

But after all, students get more opportunity to observe and judge teaching than we do. They have useful suggestions, and we should listen to them.

TAKING THE BULL BY THE HORNS: A POSTSCRIPT ON EXTERNAL PEER REVIEW OF TEACHING

The impetus for external peer review of teaching may come from departments like chemistry at IUPUI, and from forward-looking faculty like Jere Morehead and Peter Shedd at Georgia; it may also come from the disciplinary and professional societies. But individual faculty can make a dent in the issue, as well: Frances Zollers, professor of legal studies at Syracuse University, reports that she has begun requesting evidence of teaching effectiveness for candidates she is asked to review for promotion and tenure:

> "I'm often asked to serve as an external reviewer of candidates for promotion and tenure, and the dean or department chair then sends me a fat stack of material related to the candidate's research.
>
> "Recently, I've started calling back and asking for material related to teaching — something beyond student ratings. I explain the AAHE project on peer review, I talk about how it's essential to document what you're doing in teaching and how that relates to research, and so forth. . . . And in fact some candidates have teaching portfolios, and I ask to have selected entries from the portfolios sent to me. Or I may receive evidence that the candidate compiled as part of a teaching-award competition."

How well has this strategy worked? "Where the materials aren't already available," she reports, "the committee has to scramble around to put something together, and that's extra work. It's extra work for me to review the additional material, as well. But so far the departments I've dealt with have seemed genuinely pleased by my request to review not only research but evidence of teaching."

RESOURCES

Edgerton, Russell. "A National Market for Excellence in Teaching." *Change* 26 (5): 4-5 (September/October 1994).

> Responding to another article in the magazine, Edgerton argues that there's nothing *"intrinsic* to the nature of teaching and research that forever confines excellent teaching to being a local phenomenon, while research brings wide renown." He then proposes three conditions under which a national market for teaching excellence might be established: that teaching result in a visible product (i.e., be documented); that it be judged by peers; and that there be new forms of public recognition for teaching that is judged excellent.

Malik, David J. "Peer Review of Teaching: External Review of Course Content." *Innovative Higher Education* 20 (4): 277-286 (Summer 1996).

> Elaborates on Malik's report in this chapter. Issues discussed include

motivation for external review, selection of peers, dossier development, and use of results.

Mathematical Sciences Education Board. "Teaching Growth and Effectiveness: An Issues Paper." January 20, 1994, preliminary draft.

AAHE's Teaching, Learning & Technology Listserv
This electronic discussion group of 4,000+ subscribers, moderated by Steven Gilbert, director of AAHE's Technology Projects, focuses on instructional uses of technology. Some recent topics have included evaluating the impact of technology on teaching and learning, using information technology to meet the learning needs of underprepared learners, and developing support services for faculty. To subscribe, send email to:
listproc@list.cren.net
Leave the subject line blank. The text of the message should read:
subscribe aahesgit yourfirstname yourlastname

Like many of the disciplines represented in the AAHE project on the peer review of teaching, mathematics has, over the past several years, done a good deal of work aimed at raising the level of attention to teaching and its quality. This paper summarizes earlier work, sets a context for next steps, and outlines a number of possible principles and tools (e.g., teaching portfolios) faculty can use to ensure and improve the quality of teaching and learning in mathematics.

Winship, Christopher, and Mark Ratner. "Power to the Pedagogues." *The New York Times*, September 17, 1995.

Echoes Edgerton's piece (above) regarding the need for a national market for teaching excellence, but with much less optimism. Claiming that there is really no satisfactory method for evaluating teaching ("faculty members might evaluate each other's teaching . . . [but] it would take too much time"), Winship and Ratner warn that markets are more likely to recognize flashy classroom performance than real accomplishment in terms of student learning. Their conclusion: "Creating competition for Mr. Chips would be no simple matter. But it is imperative."

FROM PEER COLLABORATION TO PEER REVIEW

In his preface, Russ Edgerton points out that this volume's focus on peer collaboration originated in a shared sense among faculty in AAHE's project on the peer review of teaching that before leaping into "summative" (i.e., high-stakes evaluation) contexts it was important to experiment with strategies for being more public about teaching in ways that would serve the "formative" purpose of improvement. And our intent in the preceding nine chapters has, of course, been to provide illustrative examples of such strategies — things that faculty in a variety of settings have actually found helpful as prompts for thinking about and improving their teaching and their students' learning. It's important to say that the point of these strategies is not simply to be steps on the road to peer review; in fact, formative peer collaboration and summative peer review share a common rationale and goal, which is to make teaching more central to faculty life and more powerful in its impact on student learning. Nevertheless, it's useful, I think, in this final section, to come back around to the question of peer review, and to end with lessons about the role of faculty in the formal evaluation of teaching that are suggested by reports in the previous chapters. Four such lessons seem to me especially important.

1. We need to reexamine the relationship between formative and summative evaluation. In teaching, as in research, faculty may benefit from blurring the distinction.

Virtually all of the strategies featured in the previous chapters were originally undertaken with improvement in mind. But a good number of the Faculty Reports indicate that the same strategies were (or could be) useful for evaluative purposes, as well.

Consider, for example, Peter Shedd's report in Chapter 4, where he recounts a collaboration with his faculty partner, Jere Morehead, in which they interviewed each other's students. The purpose of doing so, as Peter points out, was to try to understand more deeply how students were experiencing their respective courses and teaching, and to gather feedback about possible improvements — which both Peter and Jere were able to make. But in addition, Peter reports, he took the initiative of writing a memo about Jere's teaching, based on the interviewing experience, with the idea, as he tells Jere, that "this just might be of benefit to you" — which, in fact, it was when Jere was nominated for a teaching award, and he chose to include Peter's memo in his application materials. As Peter says, what was originally "private between the two of us" turned out to be useful, as well, in a summative, evaluative context.

Peter's insight is echoed in reports by others: Steve Dunbar tells in Chapter 5 of developing a course portfolio in order "to know whether I'm getting through to the students." He wants, he says, "more than impressions about this." But he also intends to use the portfolio for an upcoming promotion decision: "I hope to have my portfolio put together and ready to present for review: something that will be comprehensive and data-based in a way that people haven't often seen — something the review committee can sink its teeth into." Similarly, Geoffrey Chase (in Chapter 8) tells of how "teaching development" portfolios constructed by graduate teaching assistants in the composition program at Northern Arizona University later become tools for job seeking — clearly a summative use. And the "collaborative inquiry" reported by Joy Ritchie in Chapter 7 was originally prompted by a desire to improve an important course in the program, but, as Joy tells us, she and her collaborator, Amy, will present and (probably) publish their work, where it will become a matter of public record, highly relevant to more formal evaluation.

The point of these examples is not that the formative-summative distinction is one, as they say, without a difference. No doubt about it: It's good to be clear about purposes when undertaking the kinds of processes and practices that can serve to make teaching "community property"; it's good to have ground rules at the outset about what the information will be used for, by whom, and with what, if anything, at stake. Without such understandings, contention and confusion are sure to arise.

The point, rather, is that when faculty set about making teaching "community property" in ways suggested in this book, they develop habits and practices that can, potentially, serve both formative and summative purposes. Indeed, the reports in this volume may help deconstruct what has traditionally been the gospel: that improvement and evaluation are separate and distinct, and must be kept that way. Rather, it seems, investigating and documenting one's teaching may have multiple benefits.

This, as I say, runs counter to conventional thinking, but it shouldn't perhaps be so surprising, since a similar phenomenon is taken fully for granted in research. "Consider," Lee Shulman (1995) notes, "the relationship we all had with our doctoral mentors in the dissertation. Was it formative? Was it summative? Well, you get a kind of interpenetration of the two. There's a great deal of iterative feedback, lots of suggestions, modifications, and so forth, done to make the work better and to make you smarter about doing the work. But then at some point the doctoral advisor says either 'this passes muster' or it does not. Either you are ready to defend or you are not. And in many of our institutions the doctoral advisor then becomes one of the examiners and participates in the summative review of the work." Similarly, in the research we do as mature scholars, we deliberately seek feedback from the scholarly community; we put our work forward to colleagues for their insights and contributions and critique. And we do this knowing full well (perhaps even hoping) that some of those same colleagues will judge that work in summative ways when it comes to publication, grants, promotion and tenure. . . . We cross the line between formative improvement and summative evaluation and think little of it. Indeed, doing so is part of what it means to be a member of a scholarly community — be it as researchers or (in the vision put forth in this volume) as teachers.

2. We can choose methods for the evaluation of teaching that also promote and lead to its improvement.

One of the reasons that proponents of teaching improvement have generally stayed at arm's length from its summative evaluation is because the latter is generally held to have "little correlation . . . [with] instructional improvement" (Keig and Waggoner, 1994, p. 134) and, indeed, to be a disincentive to improvement. But a second lesson from the Faculty Reports in this volume is that with a little forethought and care we might, in fact, craft evaluation processes that *also* — and powerfully — promote improvement.

A case in point is the pedagogical colloquium reported by Richard Roberts in Chapter 8. The colloquium is clearly an evaluative occasion — a very high stakes one indeed for the job candidates whose teaching abilities are being judged. But the colloquium not only results in different decisions about hiring; it also, as Roberts reports, brings faculty into conversation about departmental expectations regarding teaching in ways that are new and improvement prompting. Indeed, this seemingly secondary consequence of the pedagogical colloquium may be as important as its primary purpose.

A similar dynamic pertains in the use of teaching and course portfolios, as reported in Chapter 5: Portfolios offer more intellectually credible, authentic evidence for the evaluation of teaching (and this is their original attraction for many faculty), but along the way the process of portfolio development gets faculty reflecting on their work in powerful new ways — especially when they work with colleagues who are also developing portfolios.

The punchline here is that though the methods traditionally used to evaluate teaching have not, perhaps, done much to improve it, that situation need not be perennial . . . as Lee Shulman (1995) has argued to participants in AAHE's peer review of teaching project: "There's a principle that is increasingly employed in discussions of evaluation and assessment today — a principle that we call *'consequential validity.'* The point of the principle is that in choosing some form of assessment — of students, of faculty, of whomever — it is not enough to demonstrate that the method is accurate, that it's predictive, that it's fair — though all of those are important criteria. You also must make the argument that the use of a given method of assessment or evaluation contributes to the improvement of that which is being evaluated; that the evaluation approach advances the quality of the very enterprise being evaluated. The principle of consequential validity may help us bridge the formative/summative distinction."

In short, Shulman says, "we wish to ensure that whatever we do [to evaluate teaching] contributes to an improvement in the quality of the teaching" . . . and as many of the faculty reporting here would want to add: in the quality of student learning, as well.

3. Reflective practice and improvement should be part of what we mean by (and evaluate and reward in) good teaching.

One of the most striking (though usually unspoken) themes of the Faculty Reports in this book is the power of intrinsic motivation. The stories here are of very good teachers — teachers who have already, many of them, reaped all the available institutional rewards for teaching effectiveness — undertaking new, risky, often time-consuming processes because they find personal satisfaction in the prospect of improvement. And there is, I believe, a message here about how we define — and therefore evaluate and reward — good teaching.

Too often, the kind of teaching that's institutionally valued (though no one says this outright, of course) is teaching without visible defects — where students are satisfied, parents do not call the dean's office with complaints, and, in general, instruction is "pulled off" without apparent hitch or glitch. The extreme expression of this ethos is the feeling among faculty on many campuses that seeking assistance with their teaching (say, by visiting the Teaching Center or seeking help from a colleague) is the proverbial kiss of death.

But if we take seriously the experiences shared by faculty in this volume, a quite different conception of good teaching emerges: Excellent teaching is not "glitchless," good-enough performance; it is an ongoing, reflective process aiming always at improvement. Excellent teachers would, by this measure, be those who set out to inquire into their own practice, identifying key issues they want to pursue, posing questions for themselves, exploring alternatives and taking risks, and doing all of this in the company of like-minded scholars who can offer critique and support. These are the habits of mind we expect, after all, in scholarly work, and we should expect them in teaching as much as in research.

The corollary here is that if excellent teaching entails the deliberate pursuit of improvement, then the deliberate pursuit of improvement (I'll call it "reflective practice") should be an explicit institutional expectation when it comes to summative evaluation. Now, this is, admittedly, a point that can be taken too far: We don't want an evaluation system that rewards a bad teacher for getting a little better more than it rewards achieved excellence. But the argument embodied in the Faculty Reports in this volume is that we might in fact encourage all teachers (not just the novices and the shaky ones), at all stages of their careers, to behave as they do as scholars, seeking new challenges and issues, identifying and solving problems, gathering and using data to guide their practice, consulting with colleagues, and in general contributing to the advancement of good teaching and learning in their own classrooms and beyond.

What might an evaluation system that values this kind of teaching look like? This volume does not attempt to answer that question, but some possibilities are at least hinted at. Take for instance Bill Cerbin's course portfolio, which, as he reports in Chapter 5, contains accounts not only of successes but of several teaching activities that do *not* lead to the outcomes he seeks and which therefore force him to rethink his work. Taking a cue from this example, one might imagine guidelines for portfolio development that call for one or more entries focused on some problematic dimension of teaching — by which I mean not a "problem" or personal deficit but some aspect of teaching the field that is inherently and even universally difficult (e.g., I'm told there's a point about seven weeks into the semester in calculus where large numbers of students fall away) and which therefore *needs* the attention and good thinking of teachers willing to go public with their practice.

Even more radically, perhaps, one might imagine criteria for promotion that recognize the possibility and the need for ongoing development by faculty as teachers. At Alverno College, for instance, expectations for teaching differ by rank, with full professors being called upon not only to teach effectively in their own classrooms but to "take leadership" in assisting colleagues to teach more effectively, and to "influence the professional dialogue" about teaching and learning in higher education — expectations exactly matched to the premise of this book.

The bottom line here is that when it comes to teaching and learning, higher education suffers from a too-low level of ambition. This, I take it, is what William Massy means when he notes the inclination in teaching (but certainly not in research) to "satisfice," to make do, to be content with a certain not very lofty level of performance and to aim no higher (Massy and Wilger, 1995). The question for the future is what institutions can do to counter — rather than contribute to — this low level of ambition by explicitly calling for, evaluating, and rewarding ongoing improvement.

4. Faculty whose teaching is being evaluated should see themselves not as objects but as active, central actors in the process, generating, assembling, and putting forward for review their work as scholar-teachers.

As things now stand on many campuses, the evaluation of teaching at least feels like something that happens *to* faculty: the evaluation forms get delivered to class, filled out by students, and shipped off to the dean's office; or the department chair parachutes into class one day, checklist in hand, to conduct an observation. Indeed, even improvement — in the form of "faculty development" — tends sometimes to treat faculty as objects; as a wry faculty friend of mine put it recently — speaking from a campus that shall remain nameless — "we're developing faculty to death."

Against this backdrop, one of the most striking features of the Faculty Reports in this volume is the active agency of faculty: Virtually all are accounts of faculty taking into their own hands the responsibility to learn more about teaching, to inquire into their students' learning, to find colleagues and devise ways that they can help each other do a better job, to document and put together the case for their teaching. We take this for granted in other forms of scholarly work, and we should make it a reality in teaching, as well.

One of the arguments for the peer review of teaching is that if faculty do not seize the quality-assurance reins, "they" (legislators, the federal government, trustees, and the unwashed public . . .) will. That's an argument that most faculty acknowledge. But ultimately it is the ethical and intellectual imperative that comes through in the Faculty Reports in the preceding chapters — the need for faculty to take responsibility, as professionals, for ensuring and improving the quality of their work as teachers, which is to say, finally, the quality of students' learning, as suggested in the mission statement for the AAHE peer review of teaching project, which seems a good conclusion to this volume:

Shared Understandings

Learning. A first premise of the project is that the central goal of university teaching in the 21st century must be to teach for *understanding.* As more and more faculty are realizing, emphasis on facts, and on mastering information, must give way to more active forms of learning — forms that bring students to deep understandings, and engage them in making meaning. Progress on this difficult front means attention to the kinds of teaching that engage students more deeply and thoughtfully in subject-matter learning, and in making connections between their lives and their academic studies; it means turning classrooms into communities of scholarly inquiry in which students can be authentic participants.

Teaching. If deeper understanding by students is the goal, teaching must be seen as more than technique. A second assumption behind the project is that teaching is a scholarly activity, rooted in ways of thinking about one's field. Choices about course design, assignments given, criteria for evaluating student learning — all of these are reflections of the way the teacher understands his or her field. What's needed, then, are strategies for peer review that capture the scholarly substance of teaching, and which might therefore focus not only on what happens in the classroom (where the evaluation of teaching is now almost exclusively focused) but also on matters of *course design,* and *assessment of results in terms of student learning.*

Faculty roles. To capture the scholarly substance of teaching requires more active roles by faculty in assembling the picture of what they do, and in revealing the thinking behind the choices they make. As things now stand on most campuses, faculty are not actively involved in documenting what they do as teachers. The evaluation of teaching, for instance, seems almost to happen *to* faculty, as objects rather than as active agents in the process. But it's not enough to depend on student views to represent teaching; nor is it sufficient to drop a syllabus into a promotion and tenure file. The third assumption of the project, then, is the need for faculty to be more active agents in putting together appropriate artifacts of their teaching, along with reflective commentary that reveals the pedagogical reasoning behind them.

RESOURCES

Keig, Larry, and Michael D. Waggoner. *Collaborative Peer Review: The Role of Faculty in Improving College Teaching.* ASHE-ERIC Higher Education Report, no. 2. Washington, DC: The George Washington University, 1994.

Massy, William F., and Andrea K. Wilger. "Improving Productivity: What Faculty Think About It — and Its Effect on Quality." *Change* 27(4):10-21 (July/August 1995).

Shulman, Lee. "The Peer Review of Teaching: A Framework for Action: Three Distinctions." In *From Idea to Prototype: The Peer Review of Teaching: A Project Workbook,* edited by Pat Hutchings. Washington, DC: American Association for Higher Education, 1995.

From a transcript of Shulman's talk at Stanford during a peer review project meeting in June 1994. Located behind Tab 9.

Many faculty today are searching for more effective teaching strategies. Many are exploring new ways to involve students more fully in their learning. But what's also needed for improvement is a campus culture in which teaching is taken seriously.

What is the Teaching Initiative?

The Teaching Initiative is an AAHE program, established in 1990 with a generous gift from Allen Jossey-Bass, to help campuses improve teaching and learning by creating a "culture of teaching," an environment, that is, in which teaching and learning are the subject of serious discussion, debate, and inquiry among faculty and others committed to educational improvement. Toward this end, the Teaching Initiative:

➤ develops tools and processes that can prompt greater attention to teaching and learning;

➤ promotes a view of teaching as significant scholarly work;

➤ establishes networks for faculty and others committed to better teaching and learning.

What are its projects and lines of work?

The Peer Review of Teaching. The newest project of the Teaching Initiative is entitled "From Idea to Prototype: The Peer Review of Teaching." In partnership with professor Lee Shulman at Stanford University, and with funding from The William and Flora Hewlett Foundation and The Pew Charitable Trusts, AAHE is working with pilot departments on twelve campuses to develop processes and tools that will allow faculty to document and share what they do as teachers.

Faculty teams from the pilot departments in math, chemistry, history, English, business, engineering, music, and nursing are implementing peer review projects in their own departments, then sharing the results and implications with colleagues on their campus and, through their scholarly societies, across the country. The disciplinary and professional associations are active partners in the project.

The project is now in its second phase, and will continue through January 1998. Campus participants in this project have set up their own homepage at <http://www.AAHEpeer.iupui.edu>.

The Teaching Portfolio: Capturing the Scholarship in Teaching. Many campuses are turning to the teaching portfolio as one mechanism for the peer review of teaching. An idea borrowed from other professions (architecture, art, photography) where it has a long record of successful use, the teaching portfolio is a vehicle through which faculty members can document and reflect on their teaching effectiveness. The portfolio comprises "work samples" (syllabi, handouts, assignments, videotapes of class discussion, student papers and projects . . .) and the faculty member's commentary on those work samples (a chance to reveal the thinking behind his or her practice). Campuses using portfolios report that they not only provide more authentic evaluation of teaching but promote individual reflection and improvement.

Cases About College Teaching and Learning: Tools for Reflective Practice. Law, medicine, and business have long made use of cases to communicate and enhance professional expertise; cases about college teaching and learning can serve the same purpose for faculty. Detailed, open-ended, narrative accounts of actual teaching episodes — be it discussing *Macbeth* with a diverse group of adult students, or lecturing on the concept of evolution to a large introductory biology class — prompt powerful reflective discussion of pedagogical issues among faculty.

Over the last several years, the Teaching Initiative has sponsored scores of workshops on case writing and discussion, worked with faculty to develop cases focused on teaching in a variety of disciplines, established a clearinghouse of cases available to campuses that request them, and worked through the disciplinary associations to promote the publication of cases as a genre of scholarship about teaching. Cases also have been the focus of a four-day AAHE conference on "reflective teaching practice" held over the past several summers.

Turning Graduate Students Into Teachers. Long-term improvement of teaching may be best achieved by better preparation of graduate students for their role as teachers. As cosponsor of a biennial national conference on "The Education and Employment of Teaching Assistants," the Teaching Initiative helps bring together those involved in preparing graduate students for their work as teachers. The sixth such conference will be hosted by the University of Minnesota in the fall of 1997.

The Forum on Exemplary Teaching. The Forum on Exemplary Teaching is a special program for faculty (nearly 1,000 have now attended) held each year during AAHE's National Conference. Identified on their campuses as exemplary teachers and as leaders in the effort to improve educational quality, Forum participants share ideas about teaching improvement and ways to create a culture of teaching on their own campuses. Forum participants also serve as liaisons between their campuses and the AAHE Teaching Initiative.

What publications are available?

Making Teaching Community Property: A Menu for Peer Collaboration and Peer Review (1996) Describes nine strategies faculty can use to document and share their teaching, plus reports from faculty who have used each one.

From Idea to Prototype: The Peer Review of Teaching: A Project Workbook (1995) A 150-page binder of tasks and materials to be duplicated and used by campuses exploring new roles for faculty in the review and improvement of teaching.

The Teaching Portfolio: Capturing the Scholarship in Teaching (1991) An argument for portfolios based on a conception of teaching as scholarly work, along with sample entries by faculty in a variety of fields.

Campus Use of the Teaching Portfolio: 25 Profiles (1993) Provides accounts (two to three pages each) of how twenty-five campuses are using portfolios.

Using Cases to Improve College Teaching: A Guide to More Reflective Practice (1993).

Preparing Graduate Students to Teach: A Guide to Programs That Improve Undergraduate Education and Develop Tomorrow's Faculty (1992).

To order or to request a catalog, contact the AAHE Publications Orders Desk (202/293-6440 x11).

How can I learn more about the Teaching Initiative?

The director of the Teaching Initiative is Pat Hutchings. For further information, and to have your name added to the Teaching Initiative mailing list, please contact:

Pamela Bender, *program coordinator*
AAHE Teaching Initiative
American Association for Higher Education
One Dupont Circle, Suite 360, Washington, DC 20036-1110
ph 202/293-6440 x56
fax 202/293-0073
aaheti@aahe.org

You also can visit AAHE's homepage at <http://www.ido.gmu.edu/aahe/welcome.html> (click on "The Teaching Initiative").

What is the American Association for Higher Education?

The American Association for Higher Education (AAHE) is a national organization of more than 8,500 individuals dedicated to improving the quality of higher education. AAHE members share two convictions: that higher education should play a more central role in national life, and that each of our institutions can be more effective. AAHE helps to translate those convictions into action, through its programmatic activities, publications, and conferences. Member support enables AAHE to initiate special projects on a range of issues to create effective change at the campus, state, and national levels.

Benefits of AAHE membership include subscriptions to *Change* magazine and the *AAHE Bulletin*; discounts on registration at AAHE's conferences; discounts on AAHE's publications; and more.

"From Idea to Prototype: The Peer Review of Teaching"

In January of 1994, at its Conference on Faculty Roles & Rewards, AAHE launched a new project entitled From Idea to Prototype: The Peer Review of Teaching. In response to emerging campus recommendations — first in the 1991 "Pister Report" at the University of California, but now widely heard — that teaching, like research, should be peer reviewed, the project was designed to help campuses move toward peer review together, and to ensure faculty involvement, from the outset, in shaping strategies for peer collaboration and review that would be intellectually rigorous, appropriate to their disciplines, and practically useful in improving the quality of teaching and learning.

With two years of work completed, the project now moves into a second phase of activity. It continues to be coordinated by AAHE, in partnership with Stanford University professor Lee S. Shulman; The William and Flora Hewlett Foundation and The Pew Charitable Trusts continue to provide generous funding.

What follows here is a brief summary of the project to date and a look at plans for the next phase of activity, running through January 1998.

Context and rationale

The involvement of faculty as professional colleagues to one another in teaching, as in research, constitutes an important step forward in higher education's seriousness about teaching. During the 1970s and 1980s, clear progress was made in the evaluation of teaching; student ratings of teacher effectiveness, once the exception, became the rule, and some 86 percent of liberal arts campuses now routinely require that student ratings be used in the evaluation of teaching.[1] The 1990s, we believe, can be the decade when higher education moves to the next stage of evolution by routinely making teaching a subject for peer collaboration and review. There are four arguments for doing so:

➤ Student evaluations of teaching, though essential, are not enough; there are substantive aspects of teaching that only faculty can judge and assist one another with.

➤ Teaching entails learning from experience, a process that is difficult to pursue alone. Collaboration among faculty is essential to educational improvement.

➤ The regard of one's peers is highly valued in academe; teaching will be considered a worthy scholarly endeavor — one to which large numbers of faculty will devote time and energy — only when it is reviewed by peers.

➤ Peer review puts faculty in charge of the quality of their work as teachers; as such, it's an urgently needed (and professionally responsible) alterna-

---

[1] Peter Seldin, "How Colleges Evaluate Professors: 1983 v. 1993," *AAHE Bulletin* 46 (2): 8 (October 1993).

tive to more bureaucratic forms of accountability that otherwise will be imposed from outside academe.

On campus: advancing peer collaboration and review

For the past two years, the project has involved twelve universities working together through pilot departments — originally three on each — identified cooperatively by the campuses themselves in order to promote intercampus collaboration by field. Our goal was that historians at Wisconsin be able to work together with historians at Northwestern . . . and Georgia . . . and so forth. Faculty teams from the pilot departments then devised and implemented plans for peer review matched to their own context and purposes.

These plans, and the activities that enact them, have been deliberately varied — a corrective, if you will, to the view that peer review means exclusively classroom observation, and that its purposes must, by definition, be those of high-stakes personnel decision making. Rather, the pilot departments have undertaken peer review projects matched to their own particular purposes, culture, and needs.

In some, for instance, the goal has been to start a conversation about teaching that simply did not exist, and a successful strategy has therefore been the establishment of "teaching circles" and discussion groups. In others, more formal review has been the focus, with faculty collaborating on the design and development of course portfolios that can provide scholarly evidence of teaching for promotion and tenure decisions. A number of departments have also focused on building greater attention to teaching's quality into existing occasions and processes: for instance, asking faculty job candidates, as part of the interview process, to deliver a "pedagogical colloquium" about the teaching of their field.

During the fall of 1995, project campuses held public occasions where faculty from the pilot departments discussed their work and invited discussion and debate among a wider circle of colleagues about the issues, prospects, and possible policy implications of peer collaboration and review. In this way, relatively modest first steps are bringing larger, more lasting impact.

Larger outcomes to date

Looking across the work of the project, in its various contexts and settings, we see four significant larger outcomes to date:

Campuses Participating in AAHE's Peer Review of Teaching Project, "From Idea to Prototype"
Indiana University Purdue University
    Indianapolis
Kent State University
Northwestern University
Stanford University
Syracuse University
Temple University
University of California-Santa Cruz
University of Georgia
University of Michigan
University of Nebraska-Lincoln
University of North Carolina at Charlotte
University of Wisconsin-Madison
Additional campuses will be involved in the next phase of work

Pilot Departments
business
chemistry
engineering
English
history
mathematics
music
nursing
Additional fields will be involved in the next phase of work

1) The work of the pilot departments has helped to generate a much wider, more useful and engaging menu of strategies for peer collaboration and review of teaching.

2) Lessons have been learned and materials have been developed (see below) that can help additional campuses and disciplines begin their own efforts around peer collaboration and review of teaching.

3) Leaders from the disciplinary and professional societies have joined forces as partners in the project, working with faculty from the pilot departments to sponsor special convenings, conference presentations and colloquia, and publications focused on peer collaboration and review of teaching.

4) A lively, thoughtful conversation is now under way nationally about the idea of peer collaboration and review, and about the roles of faculty in evaluating and improving the quality of teaching and learning.

A next stage of activity

These four outcomes are, we believe, significant steps forward, but it's clear, too, that developing strategies and habits of faculty collaboration and review around teaching is a long-term agenda — and one that goes against the prevailing academic culture in many settings.

What's needed is a next stage of activity that builds on the momentum thus far established. What will it look like? Here are answers to several questions readers may have about the project's further activity and significance:

1. **Who will be involved?** Campuses active in the first phase of work will continue to work together, with coordination through AAHE. Their efforts will be aimed especially at deepening activity in the current pilot departments and extending that activity to additional departments and programs — resulting in a much expanded set of disciplinary contexts for the project nationally, as well as larger institutional impact. Special emphasis on many campuses will go to the role of the department chair.

Additionally, the project will involve new campuses and departments, through a variety of formal and informal affiliations and partnerships — our aim being both to test out ideas in different settings and to learn from places that have already made important strides toward a culture in which peer collaboration and review are practiced. Thus, for starters, the project will include several liberal arts colleges and one additional university.

2. **What roles will the scholarly societies play?** Our intention is to continue to work in partnership with the scholarly societies and other organizations whose agendas parallel those of the From Idea to Prototype project and that can help spread the word about peer review into new circles of faculty.

Toward this end, we will seed and help support related initiatives undertaken through the scholarly societies: This might mean a special issue of a journal featuring work on peer review, a convening of leaders in the field to discuss the work of faculty from the project, cosponsorship of national meetings, and so forth. We're eager to receive suggestions and proposals for work of this kind.

Second, in the fall of 1997, project activities will include meetings of fifteen-person national panels in three disciplines that have done significant work in the project — these panels designed to help key leaders in the field learn about the project, and to strategize about how the field might pursue the peer review of teaching on a national basis.

3. **What new products and resources will result?** As in the past, a major goal of From Idea to Prototype is to produce peer review prototypes and materials that can be used by faculty and campus leaders in diverse settings. Two AAHE publications on the project are currently available (see below for ordering information).

The 1995 Project Workbook is a set of materials, tasks, "think pieces," and examples that campuses can duplicate and use to develop their own parallel projects. The current volume, Making Teaching Community Property: A Menu for Peer Collaboration and Peer Review, is the second publication.

A third publication, scheduled to appear in 1996-97, will focus on the **pedagogical colloquium** (the missing half of the "job talk," focused on teaching) and other strategies for assessing teaching in the faculty hiring process. This monograph will provide examples of and practical guidance on how, exactly, to conduct a "pc," but will also explore ways that changes in the hiring process can help create a culture of teaching both in the hiring department and in the graduate programs that train new faculty.

A fourth resource will be a set of **course portfolios** in several disciplines. A small group of faculty will be working with Lee Shulman over the next two years to develop, hone, and collectively learn about course portfolios as a strategy for documenting and exploring one's teaching and student learning. The goal of this R&D effort is to produce portfolios "ready for export" — exemplars and commentary that others can use to shape their own portfolio initiatives. Portfolios will be finished at various points over the next two years, and we will work with the faculty authors and relevant scholarly societies to identify best routes for their public dissemination and discussion.

Additional documents and materials about peer collaboration and review of teaching are available on the World Wide Web homepage established by participants in AAHE's peer review of teaching project, at <http://www.AAHEpeer.iupui.edu>.

Project leadership and direction

AAHE is pleased to be undertaking this project in partnership with Lee Shulman, Charles E. Ducommun Professor of Education at Stanford University. During the 1980s, Shulman and his research team at Stanford pioneered prototypes for the evaluation of teaching in elementary and secondary schools; those prototypes are now the basis for the work of the National Board of Professional Teaching Standards. Shulman also served as chair of a university-wide committee at Stanford that recently issued recommendations for new ways of evaluating and improving teaching.

At AAHE, Pat Hutchings shepherds the project. The AAHE Teaching Initiative, which she directs, has done extensive work — and produced two AAHE publications about — the use of teaching portfolios (see p. 108 for details). She works closely on this and other Teaching Initiative projects with AAHE president Russell Edgerton and with R. Eugene Rice, director of AAHE's Forum on Faculty Roles & Rewards. Pamela Bender, program coordinator for the Forum and the Teaching Initiative, manages the daily operations of the project (and can be contacted as indicated below).

How to connect with the project

The single best venue for learning about and engaging the work of From Idea to Prototype is AAHE's annual Conference on Faculty Roles & Rewards, held in January. Workshops and sessions on peer collaboration and review of teaching are a prominent feature of the conference program each year, and the January 1998 event will serve as an occasion for *culminating project activities and dissemination,* through a major theme and program track and/or a special piggy-back event for campuses interested in tapping into the work and lessons of AAHE's peer review of teaching project.

Work from the project is also a prominent feature on other AAHE conference programs, including the annual spring National Conference on Higher Education, which includes a pre- or postconference workshop on peer collaboration and review. Additionally, we are happy to provide assistance, in the form of materials and consultation, to campuses wishing to put together their *own* events and workshops on the topic.

A variety of published resources also are (or will be) available, as indicated above. For more information about these and other AAHE publications about teaching, contact Pamela Bender, or the AAHE Publications Orders Desk at 202/293-6440 x11.

Finally, the project maintains an active mailing list for those interested in receiving notices of newly available resources and upcoming special events. To have your name added to the list, please contact:

Pamela Bender, *program coordinator*
AAHE Teaching Initiative
American Association for Higher Education
One Dupont Circle, Suite 360, Washington, DC 20036-1110
ph 202/293-6440 x56
fax 202/293-0073
aaheti@aahe.org

A final note about the AAHE Teaching Initiative

Peer review is, we believe, key to the development of a culture of professionalism about teaching; to making sophisticated judgments about the quality of teaching; to elevating the status of teaching; and to strengthening professional accountability for the quality of teaching. It is not a single mechanism or process (such as classroom visitation) but a variety of processes by which teaching can be made public, talked about, inquired into, improved, and rewarded.

In this way, From Idea to Prototype is, like all of the activities of the AAHE Teaching Initiative, aimed at helping campuses create *a culture where good teaching can thrive.*

April 1996